Green Diplomacy:

*How Environmental Policy
Decisions Are Made*

G. Bruce Doern

Policy Study 16

C.D. Howe Institute

C.D. Howe Institute publications are available from:

Renouf Publishing Company Limited, 1294 Algoma Road,
Ottawa, Ontario K1B 3W8; phone (613) 741-4333; fax (613) 741-5439

and from Renouf's stores at:

61 Sparks Street, Ottawa (613) 238-8985
211 Yonge Street, Toronto (416) 363-3171

For trade book orders, please contact:

McGraw-Hill Ryerson Limited, 300 Water Street,
Whitby, Ontario L1N 9B6; phone (416) 430-5050

Institute publications are also available in microform from:

Micromedia Limited, 165 Hôtel de Ville, Place du Portage, Phase II,
Hull, Quebec J8X 3X2

This book is printed on recycled, acid-free paper.

Canadian Cataloguing in Publication Data

Doern, G. Bruce, 1942–
    Green diplomacy

(Policy study, ISSN 0832-7912 ; 16)
Includes bibliographical references.
ISBN 0-88806-310-5

1. Environmental policy – Canada.   2. Environmental
policy. I. C.D. Howe Institute. II. Title.
III. Series: Policy study (C.D. Howe Institute) ; 16.

HC79.E5D63 1993   333.7'2'0971   C93-093193-9

Contents

Foreword

Environmental policymaking is rapidly evolving. At the global level, green diplomacy culminated in 1992 with the Earth Summit held in June in Rio de Janeiro. Canada's policy position in the international arena is the result of a complex interplay of domestic forces that do not always lend themselves to domestic consensus. Indeed, many domestic players also act on the world scene more or less independently from the domestic policymaking process. In this, Canada's environmental diplomacy differs considerably from other facets of the country's international relations. As Rio promises to have far-reaching consequences, the C.D. Howe Institute felt that an in-depth look at this unique process was required.

In *Green Diplomacy: How Environmental Policy Decisions Are Made*, G. Bruce Doern, Professor of Public Policy at the School of Public Administration, Carleton University, and a former Scholar-in-Residence at the C.D. Howe Institute, provides an overview of the players and the issues at stake and proceeds to examine the dynamics of Canadian global environmental policymaking.

This book follows on from a series of monographs and papers on environmental issues that Professor Doern has already edited or written for the Institute. *Green Diplomacy* is an important addition to that body of work, as it sets the stage for Canada's environmental relations for the rest of this decade.

The book was copy edited by Barry A. Norris and desktop published by Brenda Palmer. As with all C.D. Howe Institute publications, the analysis presented here is the responsibility of the author and does not necessarily reflect the opinions of the Institute's members or Board of Directors.

Thomas E. Kierans
President and
Chief Executive Officer

Acknowledgments

Several institutions and individuals deserve thanks for facilitating the conduct of research for this study during 1991–92. The Social Sciences and Humanities Research Council of Canada, Carleton University, and Environment Canada contributed to the funding of the research. As usual, the research and editorial staff at the C.D. Howe Institute offered constructive criticism and review. Officials in several federal and provincial departments, but especially in the International Branch of the Corporate Policy Group of Environment Canada, deserve special thanks both for their assistance in interviews and in reading earlier drafts of this manuscript. Numerous others in the broader environmental community — both environmental groups and business — also helped with interviews and comment. And my colleagues at Carleton, Glen Toner, Tom Conway, and Fen Hampson, also gave constructive help as good colleagues always do. All of the above have improved the final product, but it is the author who bears full responsibility for any remaining weaknesses in the analysis.

Bruce Doern
School of Public Administration
Carleton University
September 1992

Chapter 1

Introduction

It is not too much of an exaggeration to say that, in the 1960s, at the dawn of the modern environmental policy age, environmental issues were primarily local and regional in nature. In the 1970s, they became more clearly national in scope and involved growing bilateral relations with neighboring countries.

In recent years, however, the green agenda has become unambiguously global. As the 1992 Earth Summit in Rio de Janeiro graphically showed, the international, national, and local parameters of greening are now increasingly merged and extremely interdependent.

This is not to suggest that important international events and institutions have not always been a factor in the environmental agenda. Whether in the form of the 1972 Stockholm Conference, the Brundtland Commission of the late 1980s, or environmental accidents in places such as Chernobyl and Bhopal, international influences have always been present. What is less well appreciated in the Canadian setting and elsewhere, however, is how the international environmental decisionmaking process works and how the new dynamics involved in reaching international environmental agreements are influencing domestic policy and decisionmaking processes — including the processes used to obtain consensus, or at least to manage conflict, among increasingly diverse domestic interests.

The new dynamics of negotiation involve difficult tradeoffs among interests and regions within Canada. They embrace diverse coalitions among Western and other developed countries. And they require special "North-South" pacts between the developed and developing world over issues such as financial assistance and technology transfer provisions to ensure that the world is doing more to protect and enhance the global commons.

The purpose of this study is, first, to set out and, second, to examine the key issues and players involved in the dynamics of reaching international environmental agreements, with a special focus on the problems of forging consensus or managing conflict among the Canadian domestic interests involved.

While the study focuses on the domestic and global green policy and decisionmaking process, the notion of green diplomacy must be understood as involving integrated environment-economy decisions. In short, the dynamics of the process cannot be divorced from the larger policy and institutional issues and challenges that are inherent in global environmental concerns and in Canadian policy choices. Three such challenges continuously interact with each other: the ecological-economic challenge, the political-distributive challenge, and the managerial and organizational challenge.

In ecological-economic terms, the policy conundrum turns on how to manage a basic problem of externalities — in this case, global third-party effects — by establishing markets that will internalize environmental costs for producers and countries. Because of ill-defined or nonexistent property rights, the world's resources are extremely vulnerable to degradation. Policy problems also arise regarding issues, such as endangered species, that belong to the global commons.

In political-distributive terms, the policy issues turn on how to share the burden of change equitably and how to establish politically legitimate institutions that are capable of negotiating complex agreements and then ensuring that they are adhered to.

Finally, in managerial and organizational terms, there are policy issues surrounding the design of accountable international and domestic institutions that have the financial and scientific capacity to enable real progress to be made.

The analysis in this study deals primarily with the second and third policy challenges, and comments only briefly on the first. This is because conventional economic analysis tends to see policy problems emerging primarily from the first set of problems and too often gives insufficient attention to the second and third, more process-oriented, elements.

Set in the context of these policy issues and institutional roles, the study also analyzes five issues crucial to understanding the Canadian and international processes for reaching major international green agreements and protocols:

- the nature and dynamics of international green agenda setting — including the early warning role of science, the pressure of international environmental agencies and coalitions of nations, the leadership roles of environmental bureaucratic "policy entrepreneurs," and the media-based pressure of the international environmental interest group lobby;
- the difficult conceptual issues involved in determining what the Canadian national interest is and when it is at stake — including occasions when the Canadian approach may have to include measures to slow down international protocol-setting juggernauts[1] to ensure that domestic interests are on side and can adjust and compete in an increasingly competitive world;
- the question of the limits of domestic consensus formation arising out of the fact that a national government is elected to govern and to negotiate with other countries, and also because key interest groups have different interests and usually wish to lobby in arenas of power of their own choosing rather than just through the consensus formation machinery available for any particular negotiation;
- the issue of how to foster greater trust and confidence in the negotiation process among interest groups and provinces whose representatives are on Canada's international delegations both inside and outside the negotiating room — this includes the nature and extent of preparation of such delegations and the

---

1 By juggernauts, I mean major international environmental initiatives that develop a momentum of their own and that Canada cannot ignore.

"rules of political etiquette" involved in being a part of a national negotiating team; and

- the adequacy of the crucial relationship between the Department of the Environment and the Department of External Affairs and International Trade in coordinating negotiations, obtaining negotiating mandates and funds from Cabinet, informing Canadian interests and provinces, and securing the trust and confidence of such interests in the negotiating policies, postures, and tactics being adopted.

Given its brief length, this book is best seen as merely an initial effort to take stock of these difficult problems in the policy process and to understand who the Canadian players are. Other aspects — such as more conceptual and detailed components of the economics of environmental choice, international regime building and international organizations — are omitted. Moreover, only a few case studies in environmental decisionmaking — for example, the Convention on Long-Range Transboundary Air Pollution and the Vienna Convention for the Protection of the Ozone Layer — are examined in full, while others — such as the Rio Earth Summit and the negotiations on climate change — are discussed only by way of illustration or are so current as to be beyond proper analysis at this juncture.

The cases examined here must be set against a much longer chronology of international environmental events and agreements (see Appendix 1). Inevitably, then, the case studies in Chapters 3 and 4 involve compressed and sometimes uneven accounts of the full array of events and pressures involved. While analytical attention is paid to the interplay of interests involved in the decisionmaking process, the cases must also deal with the substantive ecological and economic issues to make sense of what happened. Other sources are cited where appropriate for readers seeking a more complete account of each case study.

The organization of the study follows the practical task at hand. Chapter 2 profiles the central policy issues and the main players and institutions involved in decisions regarding international environmental agreements and protocols. It also supplies an initial look at the typical stages in the decisionmaking process and at the provisions found in most agreements and protocols.

Chapters 3 and 4 provide a much more empirical account of actual decisionmaking processes and dynamics through an examination of case studies. In Chapter 3, the focus is first on the experience — beginning in the late 1970s and extending through the 1980s — with agreements involving the 1979 Convention on Long-Range Transboundary Air Pollution. This in turn led to protocols on sulfur dioxide, nitrogen oxide, and volatile organic compounds. Attention then shifts to the Vienna Convention for the Protection of the Ozone Layer (signed in 1985) and its resultant Protocol on Substances that Deplete the Ozone Layer (signed in Montreal in 1987). Chapter 4 moves into the 1990s and looks illustratively at some of the early dynamics involved in the complex agenda of negotiations on the Basle Convention, the 1990 Bergen Conference, the massive 1992 Rio Earth Summit, and the climate change and biodiversity conventions signed at Rio in June 1992. In these chapters, the purpose is to understand what the negotiations were about and to trace the evolution of the roles played by the main participants as new approaches to consensus formation and dispute resolution were experimented with, criticized, and adapted.

Chapter 5 presents conclusions on the policy issues that Canadians must confront and on the five key aspects of the decisionmaking process identified above. Chapter 5 also offers conclusions about the adequacy of the roles of the main players involved in contemporary environmental foreign policy.

Chapter 2

Key Policy Issues, the Players, and the Process: An Initial Profile

The processes of international green decisionmaking must first be understood in the context of the key policy issues that confront global environmental policymakers. These are introduced briefly as a backdrop to the more detailed profile of the main players and the basic stages in the decisionmaking process. The policy problems that must be faced can be seen as emerging from three basic challenges or imperatives: ecological and economic, political and distributive; and managerial and organizational.

Key Policy Issues

The ecological and economic policy issues are inevitably intertwined.[1] The overall policy goal is significantly and persistently to reduce, to control, and, in some cases, to eliminate damage to the world ecosystem caused by various single and interacting pollutants. This ultimate policy problem arises partly from the population explosion in developing countries and partly from the stark wealth that Western nations have built up through the profligate use of natural resources. More particularly, however, one of the main causes of degradation of the world ecosystem is that, in the global commons, markets do not exist that will make producers and countries fully aware of the environmental costs of decisions that adversely affect

reform

---

1 See L.K. Caldwell, *International Environmental Policy*, 2nd ed. (Durham, N.C.: Duke University Press, 1990); and D. Pearce, "Economics and the Global Environmental Challenge," *Millennium*, December 1990.

their neighbors and the world at large. This in turn requires governmental authority to establish property rights and then adequately to implement them through an array of market-based instruments and compliance tools.[2]

Within the ecological-economic policy challenge, there is the vital need to ensure that, whatever actions are taken through international negotiation and agreement, they are carried out efficiently so that the maximum resources are left for still other human problems, be they other green demands or the larger policy agenda. This has led economists to argue that international agreements on complex hazards such as global warming should be based on economic instruments such as internationally traded pollution permits and green taxes rather than on regimes based only on command-and-control regulation.[3] This would allow countries and producers to choose the most cost-effective ways of meeting the new global challenges. Indeed, economists argue that international agreements must be even more flexible than domestic regulations on the means of achieving green results.

The political-distributive elements of the policy puzzle are equally compelling. International green policies must meet some agreed test of fairness among countries and among interests and regions within countries. This is, of course, a political truism, but it is also a technical necessity in that the incidence of different hazards varies spatially and geographically within and among countries. Fairness is also required in the policies that must build and sustain the legitimacy of the international and domestic decisionmaking processes used to reach agreements.[4] This is all the more necessary in the world context because, in contrast to domestic green decision-

2　See S. Barrett, "The Problem of Global Environmental Protection," *Oxford Review of Economic Policy* 6 (1990): 68–79.

3　See M. Grubb and J.K. Sebenius, "Participation, Allocation and Adaptability in International Tradeable Emission Permit Systems for Greenhouse Gas Control" (Paper presented to an Organisation for Economic Co-operation and Development workshop, Paris, June, 1991).

4　See M. Paterson and M. Grubb, "The International Politics of Climate Change," *International Affairs*, April 1992.

making, there is no fully cohesive and established governmental mechanism — in short, there is no world government, green or otherwise. Instead, there is a world of nation-states, agreements, and, at best, a nascent capacity to make and enforce decisions.[5]

These first two imperatives, the ecological-economic and the political-distributive, combine to produce a managerial and organizational policy problem that usually then takes on, in part at least, a life of its own. Thus, international systems of accountability have to be built into the substantive policy solutions or there can be no solution. Bureaucracies must be structured to enable the design and enforcement of agreed policies. These inevitably raise issues of which countries or international agencies will have power and influence. Scientific capacity must also be built in, but kept independent from politics. In short, international greening involves the building and sustenance of sophisticated institutional capacity that is acceptable not only to governments but also to a host of other players.[6]

The Players: Domestic and International Interests

The second logical task in coming to grips with international environmental agreements and processes is to understand various stages of the negotiation and agreement process, as well as the players and interests involved. Figure 1 supplies a visual glimpse of key players whose core values, roles, and incentive systems must be mapped out, albeit statically and descriptively. Thus, we begin by profiling the key characteristics of the players arrayed on the outer circumference of Figure 1, those that interact with the Department of the Environ-

---

5 See G. Porter and J.W. Brown, *Global Environmental Politics* (Boulder, Col.: Westview Press, 1991); and O.Y. Young, *International Cooperation: Building Regimes for Natural Resources and the Environment* (Ithaca, N.Y.: Cornell University Press, 1989).

6 See F.O. Hampson, "New Wine in Old Bottles: The International Politics of the Environment" (Paper presented to the Conference on the New World Situation and the Future of Peace, Hobart and William Smith Colleges, Geneva, New York, April 27, 1991); and J.T. Mathews, ed., *Preserving the Global Environment* (London: W.W. Norton, 1991).

Figure 1: *The Players in Canadian International Environmental Decisionmaking*

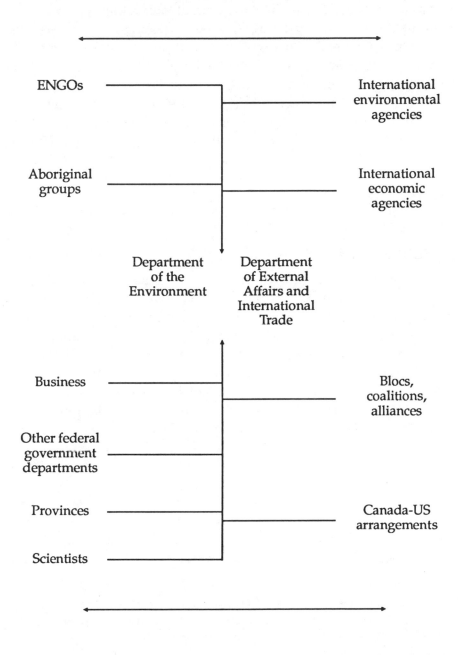

ment and the Department of External Affairs and International Trade. These two departments occupy center stage in this journey, and so the narrative builds to an eventual look at their pivotal roles. In this domestic sense, the figure is both accurate and true to scale. Almost immediately, however, one must issue a major caveat because this kind of portrait may too easily convey the notion that two pivotal departments of the Canadian federal government are in the driver's seat. With respect to the rest of the world, however, Canada's cluster of players is but one of many moving around a larger global set of players and centers of power and knowledge.[7] As one proceeds through this initial account, this larger global reality must be kept constantly in mind. In the actual case studies in Chapters 3 and 4, it will be impossible to ignore.

Domestic Interests

Box 1 on pages 12 and 13 provides a further guide to understanding the key domestic players and interests involved in the international environmental arena. For each player, the key roles and values that each tends to bring to the decisionmaking process are highlighted as well as the incentive systems and habits that often influence the strategies and tactics they adopt or prefer. In many cases, these attributes are merely extensions of observed behavior in earlier domestic environmental controversies, but they also involve habits that the later international case studies will confirm.

ENGOs

Environmental nongovernmental organizations (ENGOs) bring to the international arena the same aggressiveness and zest for the promotion and advancement of environmental values that they have domestically.[8] For them, environmental values rank highest and

---

7 See Caldwell, *International Environmental Policy*.

8 See G. Toner, "The Canadian Environmental Movement: A Conceptual Map" (Paper prepared for Carleton University, Ottawa, 1991).

unambiguously so. But ENGOs also display a vast range of philosophical and tactical positions, from the more conservative nature federations to radical ecology groups and aggressive international ENGOs such as Greenpeace. ENGOs also increasingly involve women's, labor, and youth organizations that have become a part of domestic and international consultative processes. While Canadian ENGOs have lobbied successfully in the international arena — witness the Washington campaign of the Coalition Against Acid Rain — they suffer from a lack of resources, particularly at the international level and certainly to a greater extent than do business-producer groups.

One counterweight to the ENGOs' lack of resources has been their tactical use of the media to maintain pressure on media-conscious politicians. At international negotiating sessions and meetings, ENGOs are increasingly visible and active, releasing scorecards on the participating governments with national ENGOs paying particular attention to pressuring their own country's government to do better or to adopt tougher standards or simply to not be seen as an international environmental laggard.[9]

The international arena has also witnessed the emergence of quite sophisticated international alliances among ENGOs. This is an expensive business, however, so that reliance has to be placed on well-heeled ENGOs such as Greenpeace, Pollution Probe International, the Environmental Defense Fund, and the World Resources Institute, many of which are US-based. International contact among ENGOs also varies greatly. Thus, European ENGOs talk most to each other and have less established links with US groups. Canadian and US groups deal with each other all the time, but find European contacts harder to sustain. Third World ENGOs, not surprisingly, too often find themselves badly isolated. With the collapse of communism in the former Soviet bloc, contacts between Eastern European ENGOs and those in Western countries are at last beginning to increase slowly.

---

9 See W. Lang, "Negotiations on the Environment" (Vienna, 1989, Mimeographed).

Box 1: *Domestic Interests and Their Characteristic Roles, Values, and Incentive Systems*

Environmental Nongovernmental Organizations:

- are the group most concerned about environmental values;
- have diverse philosophies on substance and tactics;
- suffer at the international level from limited resources;
- use international media to advance their cause and to pressure and, if necessary, embarrass their home government; and
- need to build links with international ENGOs.

Aboriginal Groups:

- are politically weaker than ENGOs;
- are increasingly skilled in using media;
- are even more likely to link issues to ecological unity with nature and traditional lifestyles;
- have deep concerns over land claims; and
- have an increasing role in all resource-based issues.

Businesses:

- traditionally are the most opposed to new international regimes, but the mix of business interests is changing;
- exert pressure to postpone or slow down protocol juggernauts until economics and product substitutes are right;
- may experience conflict in positions within multinational firms as they interact in more than one country's negotiation process;
- with better substitute products may break away from sectoral consensus view; and
- have difficulty forging their own consensus when the number of firms and sectors involved is large.

Aboriginal Groups

In some respects, the role of aboriginal and native groups is merely a special case of the basic situation facing ENGOs in the international environmental arena. But to treat it so would be to seriously misplace the dynamics involved. Aboriginal groups bring a particular intensity and range of environmental values to the table, in part, because

---

Box 1 – *continued*

Government Departments:

- become arenas for representing affected business sector interests;
- are concerned about the continuity of their policy roles, including their effect on foreign policy; and
- may have jurisdiction over laws that need amending to give effect to international agreements.

The Provinces:

- are opposed to being viewed as mere "stakeholders";
- see themselves as "co-governors" with Ottawa;
- may need to take action themselves if federal treaties are to be implemented effectively;
- are especially zealous in defending their natural resource ownership powers; and
- can act as representatives of powerful regional business interests.

Scientists:

- function as a fluid and complex network;
- have a less institutionalized presence than do other interests;
- play a key role at the early stage of identifying environmental hazards;
- conduct research that can trigger updates of protocol provisions;
- bring norms of objectivity and rationality to debate and analysis; and
- have a reduced role at stages of detailed protocols when other kinds of professional expertise — economic, financial, engineering, legal — take hold.

---

their centuries-long traditions and beliefs stress a unity and compatability with nature that Western cultures have tended to neglect. Aboriginal groups, too, have their own internal divisions between ecologists and conservationists, but in the main, they tend to take a much broader view of environmental issues than do nonaboriginal groups. Aboriginal groups have recently become more adept at using the international media — witness the campaigns regarding the Brazilian rain forest and James Bay — but they are still financially weak players in the long-term international environmental game.

Another special dimension of aboriginal groups in the international arena is the issue of land claims and rights. Linked both to traditional land ownership treaties and to land use, but also to claims affecting massive natural resource wealth, these groups are bound to become more involved in issues as wide ranging as forestry protocols, biodiversity agreements, hydro exports, and Arctic pollution.

Business Groups

Business groups bring to the international environmental arena some of the same values and incentives that characterize their domestic posture on environmental matters; they are, in other words, broadly skeptical. Some businesses are also ready to seek gain from better environmental rules. Of all the players, it is business that, for economic reasons, most wants to slow down the timing and effects of environmental agreements so as to protect current investment, as well as future competitiveness and market share.[10] Manufacturers of products that are hazardous and subject to international strictures usually question the validity of the scientific findings that first identify a hazard and put it on the international agenda. Their calls for more research are sometimes quite valid, but at other times this is just a tactical maneuver to delay change.

Business groups are usually more cohesive and better financed than ENGOs, and they prefer to bring pressure to bear through private channels of influence rather than overtly or directly through mass media campaigns. Business interests do, however, use the media — particularly the business press — to influence the overall climate of political opinion about the force with which green issues should and can be pressed. Since they are often suspicious of envi-

---

10 See G.B. Doern and T. Conway, *The Greening of Canada: Twenty Years of Environmental Policy* (forthcoming, 1992), ch. 5 and 9.

ronment departments, business groups are also much more likely to lobby other government ministers and departments that they feel will be more sympathetic to their interests. In Canada, these departments include Industry, Science and Technology; Energy, Mines and Resources; Agriculture; and Forestry. The Department of External Affairs and International Trade may also be an increasingly preferred channel, in part because, as Canada's trade and foreign policy department, it needs to balance economic and political concerns against environmental matters.

Since the 1980s, the solid phalanx of business interests largely opposed to environmental change has begun to break up.[11] The business community now includes at least a fourfold division of interests that may variously be involved in international negotiations. One set of interests is firms that are polluters. A second set comprises those firms and sectors that are anxious to promote a greener image for themselves or that see themselves as clean industries. A third set of interests are green industries *per se* — those whose products and process skills would profit from tougher domestic and international regulation. And finally, there are the financial, auditing, and securities industries, which are increasingly vigilant about the environmental liabilities of various sectors and firms.

A further dynamic in the business role in international negotiations is found in the division of interests that occurs among firms within a particular sector. Firms whose industrial research and development capacity has better prepared them to develop substitutes for regulated products may break ranks with their fellow sectoral members and favor tougher, rather than weaker, international rules. Other firms less capable of adaptation will be left resisting to the last or simply scrambling to keep up with the international environmental product leaders.

It is also obvious that business dynamics are influenced by the actual number of firms and sectors involved, both in Canada and

---

11 See S. Schmidheiny, with the Business Council for Sustainable Development, *Changing Course* (Cambridge, Mass.: MIT Press, 1992).

elsewhere. In the case of acid rain, only four or five key Canadian firms were involved. In the case of the ozone layer and the production of chlorofluorocarbons (CFCs), there were two Canadian producers but numerous users of CFC products. In the negotiations on nitrogen oxides, there were several industrial sectors and dozens, indeed hundreds, of firms potentially involved. It is also the case that the more international the environmental regimes are, the more that business positions must also involve hard bargaining within multinational firms. This is especially so in Canada, which has a high degree of foreign ownership. In these circumstances, while representatives of the Canadian subsidiary work with Canadian officials to hammer out a Canadian position, the parent firm is engaged in negotiations with its home country or with international agencies.

Other Federal Departments

There is always a significant amount of interdepartmental politics involved in environmental foreign policy. The broader the set of hazards being regulated internationally, the larger the number of federal government departments that could become engaged. Their engagement is triggered by at least three phenomena. The first, already referred to above, arises from the fact that affected industries are themselves likely to mobilize "their" sectoral line department, be it Energy, Mines and Resources, Forestry, Fisheries, or Agriculture, or central agencies such as the Department of Finance, the Privy Council Office, or the Prime Minister's Office.

The second trigger is jurisdictional in a different sense, in that ministers and officials of these departments will be concerned about whether an international environmental initiative will adversely or unintentionally change policy in their sphere of responsibility.

Thirdly, there may simply be legal and statutory effects in that other line departments may have jurisdiction over laws or regulations that have to be changed to give effect to Canada's international undertakings. Not unimportantly for business interests in particular, these other departments might launch their own consultative or policy review processes, which could cause a considerable stretching of resources among interest groups that have to participate in sever: consultative arenas at once.

The Provinces

In Ottawa policy jargon, all of the players mentioned so far are generically referred to as environmental "stakeholders." This includes the provinces, too, although they object strongly to being viewed in this light. The provinces do not feel that they are just another interest group, but co-governors with Ottawa in the making and implementation of environmental policy.

There is little doubt that environmental policy is *de facto* and *de jure* an area of concurrent and divided jurisdiction in Canadian federalism.[12] Foreign policy, on the other hand, including treaty-making powers, traditionally has resided with the federal government. But the extent of these powers has never been fully tested in the courts, especially since provincial statutory and regulatory changes may be required to implement treaty obligations.[13] Regardless of the legal situation, however, the political realities are such that the federal government must strive to develop some kind of basic consensus with the provinces.

Invariably, in forging that consensus, both multilateral and bilateral federal-provincial arenas must be used. Increasingly, as we will see in later chapters, the Canadian Council of Ministers of the Environment is the main multilateral arena. Bilateral negotiations occur through a variety of normal channels, depending on which provinces are most affected by, or are most crucial to, reaching a consensus.

Provincial interest in the international environmental agenda has obviously been growing in recent years, but the degree of specific

---

12 See G. Skogstad, "Environmental Policy in a Federal System: Ottawa and the Provinces" (Paper prepared for the University of Toronto, Toronto, 1991).

13 See K. Nossal, *The Politics of Canadian Foreign Policy*, 2nd ed. (Scarborough, Ont.: Prentice-Hall of Canada, 1989), ch. 9.

concern varies with the local importance of the hazard and/or with the effects that a regulatory regime might have on a regionally important economic producer and employer. Provincial interest is also intense whenever issues of the control of natural resources are involved. Since natural resources — fisheries, forestry, agriculture, oil, gas, and hydro energy sources — *are* a big part of the environment, the federal-provincial clash cannot help but escalate.

Scientists

The scientific community is unlike any of the players mentioned so far in that its institutionalized expression is less precisely identifiable.[14] Instead, it is a complicated, worldwide knowledge and professional network whose members and practitioners can be found not only in many of the institutions already surveyed but also in academe, private policy and research institutes, and international agencies.

Research findings that can place new environmental hazards on the regulatory agenda can emerge from almost anywhere. Communicated rapidly through scientific journals and conferences, these findings are vital at the front end of the negotiation-agreement process. It is only scientists — indeed, often only particular scientists — who have the knowledge and authority to tell laypersons that a hazard is a hazard. They bring to the international debate the norms of objective research and the imperatives of rational evidence.

After this agenda-setting stage, however, scientists usually become enmeshed in a more complex, knowledge-based and political-economic community that increasingly includes engineers and technologists, economists and finance experts. A wider technical and expert community begins to shape events for the simple reason that, as international protocols are actually negotiated, issues are reduced

---

14 See G.B. Doern, *The Peripheral Nature of Scientific Controversy in Federal Policy Formation* (Ottawa: Science Council of Canada, 1981).

to the practical economics of phasing down existing products and processes and replacing them with substitutes.

This is not to argue that the scientific community has no institutionalized base; bodies such as the World Meteorological Organization clearly have become more permanent forums for scientific pressure and research. Interestingly, within Canada, there is no single scientific lobby or organization known only for its environmental research and pressure. Instead, key Canadian scientific concerns have been advanced by scientific "notables" or through the ongoing work and activity of scientists in government, business, ENGOs, and the universities. Despite this more diffuse presence, there is no doubt that scientists are key players in the international environmental negotiation process.

International Institutions and Interests

The international set of players involved in environmental foreign policy is smaller in numbers than the domestic group — basically a foursome of international environmental and economic organizations, blocs and alliances, and Canada-US arrangements (see Box 2 on pages 20 and 21). This compactness, however, is in some respects misleading. This is because a full appreciation of how other countries approach negotiations would involve for each a similar mapping of the kinds of domestic players that have been traced for Canada.

International Environmental Agencies

Among the numerous international agencies that have environmental mandates, seven are important.[15] Three of them are part of the United Nations. By far the largest of these is the United Nations Environmental Programme (UNEP), which grew out of the 1972 Stockholm Conference and was initially headed by Canada's Mau-

---

15 See Caldwell, *International Environmental Policy*, ch. 3 and 4.

Box 2:   *International Institutions and*
**   *Their Roles, Values, and Dynamics***

Key Environmental Agencies — United Nations Environmental Programme (UNEP), United Nations Economic Commission for Europe (ECE), United Nations Educational, Scientific and Cultural Organization, Organisation for Economic Co-operation and Development, World Meteorological Organization, International Maritime Organization, International Union for the Conservation of Nature and Natural Resources (IUCN):

- have pro-environmental values, especially UNEP, the ECE, and the IUCN;
- have varying functions from research to policy and potentially regulatory;
- vary in membership size and hence in their degree of difficulty in mobilizing coalitions;
- are often led by people who are environmental policy entrepreneurs; and
- are extremely complex bureaucracies, especially UNEP.

Key Economic Agencies — Group of Seven, World Bank, United Nations Development Program, General Agreement on Tariffs and Trade:

- have pro-economic development values, but are beginning to be influenced by the concept of sustainable development;
- hold summits where green issues are given increasingly significant impetus;
- are a key source of environmental funding; and
- examine the use of environmental practices as trade barriers.

---

rice Strong. Its purpose is to promote international environmental cooperation, to review the world environmental situation, and to report on the implementation of environmental programs.

The United Nations Economic Commission for Europe (ECE) is composed of both Western and Eastern European countries, as well as Canada and the United States. Its mandate is broadly economic in nature, but it has become a key forum on issues such as the Convention on Long-Range Transboundary Air Pollution (LRTAP).

Box 2 – *continued*

Blocs and Coalitions — Nordic countries, European Community (EC), Group of Seventy-Seven:

- have common interests or concerns about particular environmental hazards;
- are needed to reduce negotiating process to workable groups capable of making tradeoffs on narrower issues;
- can have diverse membership — for example, both rich and less wealthy countries in the EC — and complex division of powers on green issues that makes negotiations more difficult; and
- include developing countries that insist on funding and technology transfers to alleviate pollution caused by richer countries.

Canada-United States Relationship:

- is Canada's most basic environmental relationship, despite its internationalist green rhetoric; and
- varies from cooperative (Great Lakes) to conflictual (acid rain).

The third UN arm, but the least active on environmental issues, is the United Nations Educational, Scientific, and Cultural Organization. It does, however, promote world heritage sites and other aspects of man and the biosphere.

The four other international bodies of considerable importance in environmental foreign policy are: the Organisation for Economic Co-operation and Development (OECD), the World Meteorological Organization (WMO), the International Maritime Organization (IMO), and the International Union for the Conservation of Nature and Natural Resources (IUCN).

The OECD is primarily an economic research organization of the rich Western economies, but among its many working committees there is an active one on the environment. The OECD has been especially concerned with environment-energy issues, but it has also done work on chemicals and the environment and on aspects of sustainable development. The OECD cannot make binding regulatory decisions. Instead, it seeks to persuade and educate and to develop common frameworks for viewing policy.

The WMO promotes world meteorological cooperation, information, and research, and as such is a key part of the operating context of the Atmospheric Environment Service of Canada's Department of the Environment. Indeed, both bodies evolved in the 1980s from being essentially technical and service agencies to being genuine global researchers, especially under the impetus of concerns over acid rain, depletion of the ozone layer, and global warming.

The IMO is engaged in promoting standards in marine safety and navigation, including pollution from ships. Accordingly, it is a key element in implementing agreements such as the 1973 International Convention for the Prevention of Pollution from Ships and the 1978 Convention on Tanker Safety and Pollution Prevention.

Last, but not least, the IUCN is primarily a nongovernmental body that promotes international cooperation in applying ecological concepts to the conservation and management of nature and natural resources. Its members include many governments and departments, but, as a federation of member organizations, the IUCN also includes scientific, professional, and conservation organizations from many countries. The IUCN was an important player in advancing the concept of sustainable development.

These descriptions are admittedly rather brief, but three attributes of these types of organizations warrant special emphasis.

First, they vary widely as to whether they are oriented toward research and information or have policy and potential regulatory clout.

Second, the wide variation in the size of these organizations leads member countries to calculate which agency they might want involved in an issue, either to speed up or slow down any potential international environmental initiative. Clearly, coalition-building and decision processes are much more difficult in a large organization such as UNEP than they are under the ECE.

A third feature of these kinds of organizations is that they are easily ensnared in dense thickets of international bureaucracy. But each is also staffed with ardent environmental entrepreneurs or advocates who often have surprising freedom to launch initiatives that catch member countries by surprise. The role of Mostafa Tolba, the head of UNEP, at critical junctures in the Ozone Convention process is one example of such initiative taking. Obviously, such initiatives do not occur every day, but they are frequent enough to be a potent factor in the international environmental brew, much as key senior bureaucrats in Canada have been known to be aggressive domestic policy entrepreneurs.

International Economic Organizations

Though they necessarily receive only brief mention here, key international economic organizations play a vital role in international environmental agreements, especially as they are increasingly seen as agreements on sustainable development.

The Group of Seven economic summits have given increased political impetus to the international environmental agenda. The United Nations Development Programme (UNDP) and the World Bank are key institutions in funding and financial arrangements for developing countries, and with their different views on development strategies — state-led (UNDP) versus market-led (World Bank) — there is considerable tension between the two. And trade rules and arrangements under the General Agreement on Tariffs and Trade (GATT) are becoming increasingly entwined, especially as economic interests begin to use environmental rules as new protectionist devices or seek to use trade sanctions as mechanisms to police environmental agreements even though such sanctions may be contrary to GATT rules.

Blocs, Coalitions, and Alliances

The nature of international environmental negotiations is clearly not just a straight relationship between one country and a particular international agency. The agencies themselves function in shifting blocs, coalitions, and alliances of countries, depending on the nature of the environmental problem with which they are concerned. Indeed, terms such as "blocs" and "alliances" imply a degree of permanence and stability that is much less valid for environmental matters than it has been for security matters. Moreover, in the current international context, the nature of these shifting alliances is more unpredictable than ever. In the ECE, for example, it has led to serious soul searching about how to manage economic and environmental relations. Over the past two decades as a whole, however, three blocs and coalitions deserve special mention.

In Canada's case, one important early bloc consisted of itself and the Nordic countries, especially Norway and Sweden. As smaller northern countries hit by the pollution of larger southern economies, the Nordic countries found common cause with Canada, especially on LRTAP and acid rain. Among countries such as Britain and the United States, most markedly in the Thatcher-Reagan era, the "Nords and Canada," despite their own green weaknesses, were seen as environmental boy scouts, uncomfortably progressive and a trifle presumptuous.

A second bloc of increasing importance is the European Community (EC). In international trade negotiations, the EC speaks more or less with one voice. On environmental matters, however, the division of powers between the EC Commission and the EC member states is not clear cut, so that dealing with the EC can be difficult, particularly as it now contains poorer, less environmentally conscious countries such as Greece, Spain, and Portugal.[16] The EC thus faces within its own considerably broad borders some of the same problems of coalition formation as does the international system as a whole and, indeed, as do large continental federations such as Canada and the United States.

The third bloc that merits attention consists of a group of developing countries. A "Group of Seventy-Seven" such countries has existed for some time, but is now making its presence felt on

---

16 See J. Pinder, *European Community* (Oxford: Oxford University Press, 1991), ch. 6.

environmental and developmental issues. The core position of Third World countries is quite straightforward: If the rich countries are going to cut down on pollution, most of which they are responsible for, they must not do so at the expense of the Third World's prospects for economic development. Eastern European countries share this view. Accordingly, the Group of Seventy-Seven insists that international control programs be accompanied by undertakings that there will be no net increased costs for developing countries, that the rich countries will supply new or incremental funding, and that technology transfer provisions will be a part of these funding regimes.

Clearly, the Group of Seventy-Seven is not a fully coherent voting bloc on environmental foreign policy, but there is little doubt that large members, such as China, India and Brazil, or coalitions within the bloc will have important international leverage and influence.

Canada-US Bilateral Relations

Last, but decidedly not least, in this inventory of international environmental players is the United States. Clearly, Canada has had more experience in dealing with its giant neighbor than with any other player.[17] The relationship has ranged from the successful and cooperative — for example, the Great Lakes Agreement and the International Joint Commission — to the contentious and battle-hardened case of acid rain. Between these extremes are numerous everyday problem-solving situations where a satisfactory *modus operandi* is in place.

Much as it has in its trade policy, Canada has tended to adopt an environmental foreign policy that articulates a grand internationalist and multilateral posture while keeping an eye firmly fixed on concrete bilateral relations with the United States. As long as Canada's

---

17 See P. Kyba, "International Environmental Relations: Twenty Years of Canadian Involvement" (Guelph, Ont., University of Guelph, 1990, Mimeographed); and G. Hoberg, "Sleeping with an Elephant: The American Influence on Canadian Environmental Regulation" (Paper prepared for the American Political Science Association meetings, August 30, 1990, Mimeographed).

economic and trade relations are as firmly rooted as they are in this
deep continental embrace, it is bilateral environmental relations that
will matter most, even as multilateral deals are struck.

The DOE-EAITC Nexus

As I stressed at the outset, in the Canadian context, all of these
players, both domestic and international, can be viewed as clusters
of institutions interacting with two key departments — the Department of the Environment (DOE) and the Department of External
Affairs and International Trade (EAITC) — that form the core environmental foreign policy nexus within the Canadian government.[18]
An initial sense of this nexus must therefore be understood, to be
amended and made more subtle as the case study evidence is added
in later chapters.

As Box 3 indicates, the role of EAITC proceeds from both a legal
and a political power base. Legally, the *Department of External Affairs
Act* gives the department the authority to represent Canada abroad,
to approve and accredit Canadian delegations, and to set Canadian
foreign policy in the light of Canada's overall political, economic,
and security needs. EAITC also controls the means of diplomatic
communications with other countries. Since 1982, and bolstered by
the Canada-US Free Trade Agreement, EAITC also has significant
jurisdiction on trade policy. This trade role has given the department
its own consultative entrée into the business community through a
series of Sector Advisory Groups on International Trade to an extent
that it simply did not have in earlier decades.

Politically, EAITC has always been one of the four or five most
important power bases in the federal government. And while many
other line departments add foreign policy aspects to their otherwise
domestic policy roles, EAITC has always argued successfully that,
to avoid policy chaos, it must have the final say on foreign policy.

---

18 See Doern and Conway, *The Greening of Canada*, ch. 6.

Box 3: *Outline of the Department of the Environment-Department of External Affairs and International Trade Nexus*

Department of the Environment:

- derives the legal basis for its international role from the content and logic of several pertinent statutes;
- claims particular, and sometimes unique, scientific and technical expertise on environmental issues; and
- derives its political basis from the argument that the Minister of the Environment will get the domestic political blame for things that go wrong.

Department of External Affairs and International Trade:

- derives its legal basis from the *Department of External Affairs Act*, which confers the power to make foreign policy and to approve members of Canadian delegations;
- controls the principal means of diplomatic communications with foreign states;
- derives its political basis from the argument that Canada's foreign policy would be chaotic if line departments had their own foreign policies;
- has particular legal expertise in drafting treaties; and
- is an increasingly important source of development funding through the Canadian International Development Agency.

EAITC has used both its legal and its political bases to forge its relationship with DOE. As the cases examined in subsequent chapters will show, as long as environmental issues were relatively low on the list of national priorities, as they were for most of the 1970s and 1980s, EAITC was content to maintain a careful watching brief over DOE, which it viewed as an exuberant rookie in the foreign policy field. This changed, as we will see, in the late 1980s and early 1990s. A further element of change in recent years has been the growing role of the Canadian International Development Agency (CIDA). The minister responsible for CIDA is just one of three who are organizationally part of the EAITC — the others being the

Secretary of State for External Affairs and the Minister for International Trade. But, in fact, CIDA has its own power base in that it controls a far larger discretionary budget than do the external affairs and trade elements of EAITC; it also has its own statutory base for the control of increasingly important development assistance funds.

For its part, while DOE based its international roles and obligations to some extent on a legal foundation, the more important grounds are a combined set of technical and political jurisdictional claims. On the technical power base, it was clear that DOE possessed a level of scientific expertise that EAITC could not hope to match on environmental matters. EAITC quickly conceded this obvious fact, though it claims a superior knowledge of the legal aspects of international treaties and conventions.

The political base for DOE's foreign policy jurisdictional claims is twofold. First, DOE consistently argues that it is the Minister of the Environment, not the Secretary of State for External Affairs, who must ultimately carry the burden of environmental policy failure in domestic politics. Accordingly, DOE must have a decisive role. Second, from the outset DOE saw international leadership as a key part of the moral high road that environmentalism ought to be taking. Thus, Canada's leadership role in major international environmental decisionmaking forums was always significant. Indeed, many DOE officials, usually scientists, became international environmental policy entrepreneurs in much the same style referred to earlier in the discussion of international green bureaucracies.

Key Stages in the Decisionmaking Process

In addition to an initial profile of domestic and international interests, it is also vital to have a sense of the basic stages of the international decisionmaking process and of the content typical of international agreements, conventions, and protocols.

An agreement could be something as basic as a statement agreed to among ministers. For example, the 1984 meeting of the

"30 Percent Club," a group of states committed to significant reductions in sulfur dioxide emissions, resulted in an agreement, but it was not a convention or a protocol. A convention is a much more formal international pact whereby the signatories commit themselves to a long-term set of principles and some initial actions. Some early environmental conventions actually contained many detailed provisions, but as issues have grown in complexity, conventions have tended to become broader framework deals. One or more protocols are then later negotiated under which even more precise commitments are given, backed up by a regime of implementation and sanctions.

As Box 4 shows, the decisionmaking process begins with the identification of an environmental problem or hazard. This stage typically is dominated by the findings of scientists, and it can go on for several years while scientists debate and political and economic interests decide how far to push for, or resist, solutions. This is followed by the formal international political recognition of the problem, including a United Nations General Assembly resolution to negotiate a convention. Other discussions lead to agreed statements of concern by various countries and agencies, and eventually negotiations begin on the formal international convention.

Again, the convention stage can take several years. Negotiations usually center on just how general or specific various countries' commitments should be. The focus here is also on devising a set of workable principles. The more that one proceeds into the protocol-setting stage, the more that concrete domestic interests are likely to be involved.

Before going on to the negotiation of a formal protocol, a process occurs that is best described as the development of regulatory and control mechanisms. These usually have to be thrashed out in complex technical and policy meetings to obtain a good practical sense of the kind of control regime that is needed and that is likely to work.

At the protocol stage, and at earlier stages as well, attention must be paid not only to formal negotiating sessions but also to the

---

Box 4: *Typical Stages in the*
Green Decisionmaking Process

1. Early awareness and scientific identification of hazard.

2. Global recognition of problem.

3. Convening of meetings to develop a convention.

4. Development of major ministerial statements of concern.

5. Development of convention: actual negotiating sessions; between-negotiations study and lobbying.

6. Development of strategy for regulation and control.

7. Development of protocols: actual negotiating sessions; between-negotiations study and lobbying.

8. Development of control measures.

9. Development of funding mechanism.

10. Implementation: signature; ratification; entry into force.

11. Enforcement.

12. Built-in review, feedback, and discovery of links to related or new hazards and pollutants.

13. Renegotiation of treaty.

---

numerous interim meetings of lawyers and technical and economic experts. These groups hammer out the agreed data bases, formulas for reducing or controlling emissions, and time frames for achieving goals.

At the ultimate negotiating sessions, domestic interests increasingly want to ensure that they are represented on the accredited negotiating team — preferably in the room and at the table. If not in the room, then they certainly want to be in the next ante chamber, cattle prod in hand, to encourage the chief negotiator as required. Alas, the image of a few individuals sitting around a table in a cozy room is a false one, as delegates soon discover. The standard negotiating room is, in fact, a very large space containing dozens of delegations.

Ultimately, negotiations are likely to devolve to a small gathering of key players who are proxies for the various geopolitical blocs whose shape will have become evident from earlier meetings. The role of the host country is often vital in this regard, in part because the home government's prestige is visibly on the line in front of its own citizens and media. A demonstrable success, or at least symbolic gestures of success, must be seen to emerge.

The role of the media at the negotiations is also an important dynamic because the national and international ENGOs increasingly present at such meetings rely on the media to pressure delegations to commit to environmentally progressive positions and to show them up if they fall behind in the world league of environmental achievement.

The role of the media, however, is by no means confined to the negotiating phase. At the very earliest stages, when scientists are raising concerns, the media are crucial. In later stages, the media are often important means by which national authorities can be held accountable for their international commitments.

After a protocol has been negotiated, the decisionmaking process goes through a series of potentially lengthy steps. The first step is for a country to affix its signature to the convention or protocol — like a premarital engagement, it acts as an indicator of serious intent. The second step is formal, legal ratification, which, among other things, ensures that a country has put in place the necessary statutory changes to give effect to its commitments. This is followed by the entry-into-force stage: Agreements do not take effect until the minimum number of countries with appropriate shares of production have ratified. Enforcement, evaluation, and review then follow, processes that are intended to ensure not only that commitments are actually honored but that momentum for the advancement of environmental change is maintained. Through a process of obligatory review and study, with fixed review periods built in, links between new research findings and new control regimes are identified, and

---

Box 5:   *Typical Provisions of Environmental Agreements and Protocols*

- Statement of principles;
- provision for national strategies and studies;
- funds and technology transfer mechanisms;
- institutions;
- mechanisms for implementation and enforcement; and
- provisions for monitoring, review, and updating.

---

new or related hazards are discovered. Potentially, this leads to renegotiation of the treaty to improve its stringency and operation.

The implementation of agreements, like most policy implementation, requires actions by numerous interests, both public and private. One can derive a partial sense of the difficulties — and yet the vital nature — of this, the least visible part of the decisionmaking cycle by looking briefly at the increasingly typical content of major international environmental agreements. As Box 5 suggests, such agreements usually contain a statement of principles that set out the common ground for the signatories' thinking.[19] Typically, there are also sections requiring the development of each signatory's own national strategies, including the publication of studies to help establish appropriate data for comparison.

Agreements also have to contain funding mechanisms, which, in turn, are often linked to the issue of easing the transfer of the best available technologies to those countries that have older or environmentally inferior production technologies. Developing countries, as noted previously, have insisted on the use of such funds and transfer mechanisms.

---

19 See W.A. Nitze, *The Greenhouse Effect: Formulating a Convention* (London: Royal Institute of International Affairs, 1990).

It is a short step from these sorts of provisions to the realization that complex institutional modifications or, indeed, entirely new institutions must be designed if countries are to agree on funding ceilings and formulas, administer funds, obtain data and report on implementation, and carry out further research. These issues accordingly make up a large part of any protocol document.

Conclusions

To understand how international environmental agreements are reached, one must first have a good sense of the key policy issues at stake and the players involved on both the domestic and international sides of the decisionmaking equation. One also needs an initial sense of the basic stages involved in the decisionmaking process and the typical kinds of provisions environmental agreements contain. The account so far has been an essentially descriptive one. In the realm of policy issues, a trio of policy imperatives competes for attention as negotiations evolve:

• the ecological-economic imperative involves the setting of standards to sharply reduce global pollution, and the use of flexible economic instruments to ensure the efficient adaptation to a greener sustainable economy;
• the political-distributive imperative requires that international regimes distribute the costs and benefits fairly, both among nations and among interests within nations; and
• there are vital managerial and organizational policy issues involved in the establishment of accountable, and financially and scientifically effective, institutions.

Each of the players in the process brings a different, partially conflictual and partially complementary, set of values to the table. And each is known to prefer certain tactics arising from the incentive systems that characterize the institutions or sectors of society in which they function.

Chapter 3

The Dynamics of
Green Diplomacy in the 1980s

The period from the late 1970s to the late 1980s marked the emergence of several important international environmental agreements. This chapter looks at two case studies of green decisionmaking processes and dynamics: the 1979 Convention on Long-Range Transboundary Air Pollution (LRTAP), and the 1985 Vienna Convention for the Protection of the Ozone Layer. The analysis also deals with some of the protocols that emanated from these conventions — namely, the 1985 sulfur dioxide (SO_2) and 1988 nitrogen oxide (NOx) protocols from the LRTAP Convention, and the 1987 Montreal Protocol on Substances that Deplete the Ozone Layer — especially chlorofluorocarbons (CFCs) — that resulted from the Ozone Layer Convention.

In each case, the format for the analysis is to trace the basic chronology of the events and pressures involved, and to examine and characterize the roles of the players involved. The goal here, as throughout the study, is to understand what kind of institutional learning was going on and how well domestic consensus and conflict was being managed.

The Dynamics of the
LRTAP Convention and the
SO_2 Decisionmaking Processes

The LRTAP issue, initially associated with acid rain but in fact involving several related pollutants, was first propelled onto the international agenda by scientific findings.[1] These emanated from work undertaken as early as 1973 by an LRTAP committee of the Organisation for Economic Co-operation and Development (OECD), as well as from research by Norwegian and Swedish scientists.[2] Atmospheric research work in Canada's Great Lakes area was also pivotal.

The Scandinavian research showed that long-distance boundary fluxes of SO_2 were a major source of acid rain in Europe, most of it coming from Britain and West Germany. Scientists in Canada's Department of the Environment (DOE) were aware of these research findings and began to press the issue when the Great Lakes atmospheric research showed similar damage in Canada.

In May 1975, a major international symposium held in the United States brought the seriousness of the research, including its application to North America, to broader light. In 1976, the Science Council of Canada made acid rain one of the five hazards it examined in its *Policies and Poisons* study.[3] In August 1976, DOE established an integrated research program on LRTAP.

Aside from this important scientific impetus, at least two political dynamics edged the agenda toward the signing of an international agreement. First, the Soviet Union, in the context of the Helsinki Accord on East-West cooperation, decided to make the environment an area for such cooperation. The problem was how to activate environmental initiatives. The OECD had excellent research credentials, but it was not a decisionmaking body and did not include Soviet and Eastern European countries. The United Nations Economic Commission for Europe (ECE) was more political in nature,

---

1 For a more detailed account of the Canadian SO_2 and acid rain story, see G.B. Doern and T. Conway, *The Greening of Canada: Twenty Years of Environmental Policy* (forthcoming, 1992), ch. 8.

2 See Organisation for Economic Co-operation and Development, *The OECD Programme on Long Range Transport of Air Pollutants* (Paris, 1977); and *Ecological Impact of Acid Precipitation* (Proceedings of a conference held at Sandefjord, Norway, March 11, 1980).

3 See Science Council of Canada, *Policies and Poisons* (Ottawa, 1977).

but it could reach decisions, and quickly became the regional focus for transboundary air pollution issues.

The second political impetus came from the other side of the Atlantic. In November 1978, the US Congress passed a resolution enabling the Carter Administration to discuss with Canada its concerns about the effects of Canadian air pollution emissions on the United States. Specifically, some congressmen were concerned that a proposed coal-fired plant being built in northwestern Ontario would spread acid rain into Minnesota. Canadian officials jumped at the chance for such talks, and a Bilateral Research Consultation Group was set up to integrate North American research on LRTAP. Its first report in 1979 reaffirmed the seriousness of the acid rain problem in North America, noting in particular the effects of US emissions on Canada.

In 1979, a convention on LRTAP was negotiated in Geneva. It did not contain any specific obligations to reduce emissions, primarily because of opposition from Britain, the United States, and West Germany. Instead, the convention merely required the parties "to endeavour to limit and, as far as possible, reduce and prevent air pollution." While there was great dissatisfaction in Canada and Scandinavia about the relative lack of progress, DOE was still focused on the Canada-US bilateral arena.

In particular, DOE was worried about declining US political interest in the issue and the increasing stalemate in Congress. During 1980, Canadian strategy was to press the Americans to move closer to some kind of agreement for joint action.[4] In August 1980, with the Carter Administration still in power, Canada secured the signing of a Memorandum of Intent that set out the two countries' mutual goal to take concrete cooperative steps to combat acid rain. When the Reagan Administration came to power in 1981, however, the acid rain issue died politically. Indeed, environmental issues as a whole simply were not a priority of the Reagan presidency. By June 1982,

---

4 For a full account of the acid rain case, see Doern and Conway, *The Greening of Canada*, ch. 8.

acid rain talks had broken down, and Canada expressed its anger in language that was quite undiplomatic.

While some further meetings occurred with the United States, Canada's strategy necessarily shifted back to the multilateral arena. The Department of External Affairs, at this stage, was counselling patience in dealing with the United States and preferred a traditional diplomatic approach. The strategy, as forged by the previous environment minister, John Roberts, committed Canada to reducing its acid rain emissions by 50 percent, with half of this reduction undertaken unilaterally and the rest linked to parallel US actions. Initially, the provinces were left to pursue the domestic portion of this commitment. It was not long, however, before DOE officials, as well as a very determined new minister, Charles Caccia, had begun to devise a strategy to seize the federal initiative over lagging provincial actions. The new strategy also led to the formation of the "30 Percent Club" — a group of countries, mobilized by Canada, committed to reducing SO_2 emissions by 30 percent by 1993. In effect, by 1983, the negotiations on an SO_2 protocol had unofficially begun.

At this point, the dynamics of the negotiations took on an array of features linked both to personalities and to alliances. Canada was a leader in forging a coalition with the Nordic countries in part because DOE's minister was prepared to run hard with the issue. Key DOE officials, such as Jim Bruce, then Assistant Deputy Minister of the Atmospheric Environment Service, and Danielle Wetherup, then Director of Intergovernmental Affairs, both freelanced, in the sense that they moved on their own to extend their contacts with other key players abroad. Canada then greatly angered the United States by maneuvering Bruce, with Swedish and Norwegian support, into one of the cochair positions of the key ECE committee that would examine SO_2. The other cochair was a Soviet representative with whom Bruce developed an excellent working relationship. As the various meetings were held and as different pressures were applied, alliances both shifted and took hold.

Canada and the Nordic countries, motivated by the fact that they were most affected by acid rain from sources in large neighboring countries and confident about the quality of their research on the issue, formed the core alliance favoring action on SO_2. Most opposed were Britain and the United States, two of the largest polluters. These two countries became convenient environmental villains in the media, roles made all the more plausible by the unabashed pro-market, anti-environmental stances of the Thatcher and Reagan governments.[5]

Circling around this core of protagonists was a more fluid array of countries whose attitudes reflected the degree to which they were contributors or victims of SO_2. West Germany became a key swing player, opposed to action at first but then moving to a more support-ive role when research showed massive damage to the Black Forest and when Green parties rose to political prominence. France, Bel-gium, and even the Soviet Union gradually began to side with the Canadian-Nordic alliance.

Canada's initiative to form a 30 Percent Club bore fruit in 1984. Environment Minister Charles Caccia held a meeting of the club — well covered by the media — on March 22 at which Canada and nine other countries signed a declaration of their intention to reduce SO_2 emissions by at least 30 percent by 1993. This target was not a problem for Canada because it had already committed itself to reductions of 50 percent by 1994 in the seven easternmost provinces. The club eventually expanded to 22 countries, and its members signed the ECE-sponsored Helsinki Protocol on SO_2 in July 1985.

While DOE was justifiably proud of its environmental leader-ship, the victory was a hollow one and somewhat a political side-show since neither Britain nor the United States signed the Protocol. What mattered most to Canada, after all, was whether the United States would take action and whether the provinces would meet their part of the bargain. As it turned out, the United States took no action until the passage of amendments to the *Clean Air Act* in 1990.

---

5 For the European story on acid rain and SO_2, see S. Boehmer-Christiansen, *Acid Politics* (London: Oxford University Press, 1990). For the US dynamics, see J.L. Regens and R.W. Rycroft, *The Acid Rain Controversy* (Pittsburgh: University of Pittsburgh Press, 1988).

Thus, in some respects, events in the multilateral arena tell only a small part of the story. To appreciate fully how green diplomacy developed in the 1980s, one has to look at domestic Canadian environmental strategy and at Canada's green relations with the United States.

As noted earlier, Canada's strategy on acid rain until 1984 involved reducing emissions by 50 percent in conjunction with parallel US actions. This strategy made considerable sense, not only in terms of bargaining with the United States but also because some of the hardest-hit areas in Canada — such as Ontario's Muskoka region — were being polluted by emissions from the United States, notably the Ohio Valley. Thus, even a strong Canadian control program would have had only limited effects in some areas.

For its part, the United States responded by arguing that Canada had to show scientifically that there was in fact a problem. Moreover, the United States insisted, Canada had to show its environmental *bona fides* by taking appropriate domestic action to control emissions if Congress was to be impressed. But the US position was also the product of the complex set of political interests involved in the US acid rain battle.[6]

In the 1970s, when Canada and the United States cooperated on Great Lakes water pollution, the politics of US state governments were fairly simple: On water issues, the states that were the sources of the pollution were also its victims. In the case of acid rain, however, the sources of the pollution, Midwestern states with coal-fired power plants, formed a politically distinct coalition from those areas — New England, New York, and Pennsylvania, for example — on which the SO_2 emissions fell. Another complication was the difference in the primary causes of acid rain in the two countries: smelters in Canada, and coal-fired power plants in the United States. This, in turn, affected the nature of the coalitions involved. In Canada, the producers consisted of a small handful of key firms such as

---

6 See Doern, *The Greening of Canada*; and Regens and Rycroft, *The Acid Rain Controversy*.

INCO, Ontario Hydro, Falconbridge, and Algoma. In the United States, the producers were the more numerous power-generation companies, as well as influential coal producers and their powerful unions. These differences also influenced the nature of control approaches and mutual arguments about environmental virtue. For example, US regulations required the installation of expensive scrubbers on coal-fired plants. Canada had no similar requirements, a fact which US interests used to argue that Canada was insincere in its approach. In Canada, with its polluting smelters, each of the principal companies had different production mixes and technologies.

The coalitions that formed in the United States were quickly replicated within Congress, making a Canada-US deal even more difficult. Political gridlock developed among pro-environment interests and regions, those ardently opposed to acid rain action, congressional interests that were neutral, and an anti-environment Reagan Administration that was content to see the gridlock prevail. The 1982 recession, which bludgeoned key Midwestern states, only served to make the situation worse. In this setting, US coal interests pulled no punches, campaigning against acid rain controls and opposing Canadian electricity exports. Indeed, they went so far as to accuse Canada of using its demands for acid rain controls as a kind of protectionist Trojan horse to expand electricity exports.

But while Canada tried to take the environmental high ground, its own domestic record of controlling emissions was sluggish until the mid-1980s. In April 1981, the federal government and four provinces had committed themselves to holding acidic deposition loadings to an initial target of no more than 20 kilograms per hectare per year by 1990. It was not until February 1985, however, that an actual control program was announced, committing the federal government and seven easternmost provinces to reduce annual emissions of SO_2 by 2.3 million tonnes, a 50 percent reduction from 1980 allowable levels, by 1994. A month later, the federal Cabinet approved an acid rain abatement program that included a $150 million financial support package for smelter modernization. By the end of 1985, the Ontario government had announced its own $85 million

Countdown Acid Rain Program, matched to an equivalent federal amount, which would cut emissions in the province by 67 percent.[7]

These Canadian actions could not have happened until several political ducks had been properly aligned and some opportunities for symbolic environmental politics had been exploited. During this 1984–85 period, these included:

- the autumn 1984 election of a Conservative federal government;
- the first "Shamrock Summit" between Prime Minister Mulroney and President Reagan, the prospect of which freed up money to finance the smelter modernization program;
- the election of a Liberal government in Ontario that was anxious to advance environmental reform and to show some environmental and partisan one-upmanship with respect to the federal Tories; and
- the gradual working out of a regulatory *modus vivendi* and incentive package to suit each of the key polluting companies.

It took all of these events to tip the scales domestically, but the most crucial was the positions of the companies themselves.

From the outset, the key companies involved, especially in Ontario, opposed a controls program for all the usual economic reasons. If there was to be one, they insisted that it be tailored to each firm's different production and investment situations. These firms — INCO, Falconbridge, Algoma, and Ontario Hydro, which accounted for more than two-thirds of Ontario's SO_2 emissions — had considerable clout in the counsels of the Ontario Conservative government, which, in the late 1970s, was ending its third decade of continuous power.

One catalyst for change was the severe 1981–82 recession, which caused a considerable amount of soul-searching in the mining and smelting industry as a whole. In 1983, a cooperative business-

---

7 See D. Dewees, "The Regulation of Sulphur Dioxide in Ontario," in G.B. Doern, ed., *Getting It Green: Case Studies in Canadian Environmental Regulation* (Toronto: C.D. Howe Institute, 1990), pp. 129–154.

government study was launched to look at the entire world compet-itive situation of the Canadian industry.[8] Since this review involved a close examination of new production technologies, it provided an opportunity, arguably for the first time, to relate environmental matters to these new or probable future investment choices. The industry made clear to Ottawa, however, that if it wanted to piggy-back environmental issues on the new policy and regulatory mix, then it would have to help pay for the environmental modernization program.

Even under these circumstances, however, the position of each firm clearly would be different. Falconbridge, for example, had recently modernized its smelters and so it argued that it was now up to others to catch up. In Quebec, Noranda argued that it could not afford to pay and therefore federal assistance was mandatory. For its part, INCO was quite skeptical about possible change, but eventu-ally became enthusiastic when it saw that it could profit from the new technologies it would use.

Eventually, after much tough bargaining — including different federal-provincial battles over precise funding packages — a control program was put in operation. Meanwhile, action on the US front continued to be delayed, in part by the politics already sketched above and in part by the tactical use of the politics of science. The latter referred to the frequent denigration of the findings of even independent scientists by political operatives in the Reagan White House. For its part, Canada had little choice but to agree to the Davis-Lewis Special Envoys report of January 1986.[9] This report did lead to an important US investment in demonstration technologies, but the Canadian media generally saw it as evidence of Canadian delay and lack of influence in US political circles.

The only player whose role has not been referred to thus far is the environmental nongovernmental organizations (ENGOs). In the

---

8 Canada, *Canada's Non-Ferrous Metals Industry: Nickel and Copper* (Ottawa: Supply and Services Canada, 1984).

9 D. Lewis and W. Davis, *Joint Report of the Special Envoys on Acid Rain* (Ottawa: Supply and Servicesn Canada, January 1986).

LRTAP Convention process, no Canadian ENGOs were in the room. International ENGOs were, however, involved: Greenpeace and the International Union for Conservation and Nature (IUCN) were present at Geneva and Helsinki, both in the room and in utilizing media pressure in the halls. Relative to later campaigns, however, this was a fairly modest and low-key affair, especially for Greenpeace.

The involvement of Canadian ENGOs was limited in part by their financial resources. The DOE negotiators contracted the National Survival Institute to provide a newsletter for other ENGOs on the issue, but this was the extent of active multilateral involvement. Limited participation was also due to the simple fact that Canadian ENGOs saw the multilateral arena only as a sideshow. Instead, their energies were focused on the Canada-US arena. And here the key ENGO was the Canadian Coalition on Acid Rain (CCAR).[10] Established in 1980, partly with the encouragement of former environment minister John Fraser and funded partly by DOE funds, the CCAR was one of the first Canadian groups whose avowed purpose was overtly to lobby the US Congress and US public opinion rather than just the US Administration. It also, of course, lobbied hard on the Canadian side of the border.

There is little doubt that the CCAR kept up the pressure on politicians and increased Americans' awareness of the acid rain problem. For its part, DOE regarded the CCAR as a mixed blessing. On the one hand, the Coalition was essential in keeping the acid rain issue alive. On the other hand, DOE often found itself putting out diplomatic fires or having to keep options open as both it and then the CCAR would buttonhole the US Administration, often on the same day but with different messages about Canadian positions. DOE also viewed the fact that the CCAR was very critical of the Canadian record as reducing Canada's already limited leverage on the United States.

From a Canadian perspective, one could give a mixed verdict on the overall LRTAP Convention and SO_2 Protocol decisionmaking

10 See Doern and Conway, *The Greening of Canada*, ch. 5 and 8.

processes. Canadian scientific preparedness was good and, in a process that was fairly new, Canada exercised considerable leadership. Canada had to wait, however, until the domestic political ducks were lined up, with respect to both the key handful of firms and the main provinces, especially Ontario. Most important of all, Canada lacked sufficient leverage in the United States, which did not take action until interest groups and congressional politics there allowed it to occur and until an Administration came to power that was prepared to try to break the congressional gridlock.

And Then There Was NOx: How Not to Set Protocols

The second protocol to flow from the LRTAP Convention was the Protocol on nitrogen oxide emissions, signed in Sofia, Bulgaria, in October 1988. NOx emissions come primarily from the combustion of fossil fuels in energy generation and automobiles.[11] Emitted primarily in the form of nitric oxide, they are rapidly converted into nitrogen dioxide. NOx emissions are also linked to emissions of volatile organic compounds (VOCs), on which a further protocol was also being negotiated. VOCs are released during combustion from various industrial processes and from the evaporation of liquid fuels, solvents, and organic chemicals. The secondary and combined effects of NOx and VOCs pollutants in the form of ground level ozone, a component of urban smog, was also a central Canadian concern. While our interest here is with the NOx Protocol, it should be emphasized that the LRTAP agenda included several interacting pollutants, the existence of which altered the technical, economic, and political composition of the negotiations.

The Sofia Protocol requires the signatories to freeze NOx emissions at their 1987 levels by 1994. They are also required to develop future targets, to begin in 1996, for the reduction of NOx emissions.

---

11 See Long Range Transport of Air Pollutants Steering Committee, *Management Plan for Nitrogen Oxides and Volatile Organic Compounds* (Ottawa, March 1990).

These targets are to be based on the concept of the "critical load," which is basically the point "at which a specified receptor in the environment begins to be damaged by the presence of a pollutant."[12] In practice, this means that each country has to assess the ability of its different ecosystems to handle the pollutant and then to establish appropriate targets for the reduction of NOx emissions. The signatory countries were also enjoined to employ the "best available technologies which are economically feasible" to reduce NOx emissions from major new stationary and mobile sources.[13]

From the Canadian perspective, the dynamics of the NOx decisionmaking process were quite different from those of SO_2.[14] As pointed out above, the NOx hazard had always been part of the LRTAP agenda, and scientists had recognized and identified the hazard quite early on. But the journey from initial identification to its focus as a key part of a protocol is not a simple one.

In September 1986, West Germany, Switzerland, Austria, and several other countries — under domestic pressure from their Green parties — began to develop standards on NOx emissions, especially from autos, that were still weaker than those of Canada. Many of these countries did not have a good environmental image abroad, and new evidence showed that their forests were deteriorating badly, in part due to their own NOx emissions. Along with the Nordic countries, they attempted to pressure Canada and some other countries into forming yet another 30 Percent Club, this time to reduce NOx emissions by 30 percent.

This was one 30 Percent Club, however, that DOE decided, for good reasons, it did not want to join. First, the European countries with the worst records were seeking a 30 percent reduction from a high emissions base. It made for good environmental rhetoric in the home political market, but for countries that already had better

---

12 See Canada, Department of the Environment, International Affairs Branch, "Critical Load versus Percentage Reduction," *Briefing Note*, January 1989, p. 1.

13 Ibid.

14 See G.B. Doern, "Regulations and Incentives: The NOx-VOCs Case," in Doern, ed., *Getting It Green*, pp. 89–110.

environmental records, further 30 percent cuts were far more difficult and might not have made sense relative to action on other pollutants. But for a country to say that it opposed such targets risked running into problems with environmentally conscious media. DOE spokespersons attempted to defend Canada's position by likening it to asking a fat person and a thin person both to lose 30 percent on a diet.

A second reason was that the negotiation of international control regimes invariably involves a range of technically complex instrumental and conceptual choices, from the adoption of ceilings on emissions to percentage reductions to the adoption of best available technologies to critical loads. These, in turn, require technical precision in the context of the particular array of hazards involved.

At the end of the SO_2 episode in the mid-1980s, Canada's international environmental credentials were very good. In the SO_2 case, Canada had been a leader and had developed a good scientific base for its policy positions. Moreover, its negotiating positions were not crucial to its domestic control programs in that they already exceeded its international obligations. But NOx was a different and more complex matter.[15]

DOE scientists did not know to what extent NOx was a serious problem for Canada's forests. Knowing the impact of extreme NOx emissions, as was the case in Europe, was a scientifically different and less difficult problem than knowing the impact of low NOx emissions, which was the situation in Canada. DOE scientists did know that, in Canada, the combination of NOx and VOCs was causing the problem of urban smog, but the seriousness of the problem varied widely across the country. It was clear again, therefore, that it was not going to be in Canada's interests to agree to across-the-board percentage cuts.

But there was more to the NOx story. During the negotiations on the reduction of NOx emissions, pressure from ENGOs, publicity

---

15 The contrast between the two situations was acknowledged in a brief DOE paper on the subject. See Canada, Department of the Environment, International Affairs Branch, *International Environmental Issues: A Status Report* (Ottawa, 1990).

by the mass media, and anxiousness on the part of DOE to use the NOx issue to keep international pressure on the United States on the larger transboundary bilateral issues all combined to create a potent brew that energy interests saw as "act now, think later." The brew was aided and abetted by the oppressive heat of the summer of 1988 and the attention the media paid to the issue of global warming.

By the later 1980s, Canadian and international ENGOs were even more impatient for change. The NOx meetings were not exciting events, however, and did not attract the media to the extent that the acid rain issue had. Nonetheless, one of the ENGOs at the meetings issued a report that was extremely critical of Canada's NOx role. The Canadian media present reported on this assessment and brought additional pressure to bear. The story then hit the Toronto media, which led to interviews with the Ontario Liberal environment minister, who argued that Canada ought to join the latest 30 Percent Club.

This mixture of international embarrassment, federal-provincial one-upmanship, and scientific uncertainty need not have resulted in precipitous action by Canada, but it did. Canada supported a NOx protocol that went further than key energy interests could tolerate. There were also divisions of opinion within DOE itself about how to deal with the NOx issue. Some officials felt that Canada was not technically ready to deal with NOx issues, while others were eager to put additional pressure on the Americans.

It is important to note here that two different forces were at work in these situations. On the one hand, the NOx issue was like a new environmental train of progress leaving the station, and DOE did not want to be left behind. On the other hand, there was DOE's growing frustration with the Reagan Administration's reluctance to deal with environmental issues. Even though the SO_2 case had shown that real leverage on the United States was very difficult, some in DOE thought that the NOx Protocol could keep up the international pressure.

Some business interests and provinces felt that the NOx decision-making process contained few of the prior warnings and domestic massaging that had preceded the SO_2 issue. They were vaguely aware that negotiations were under way, but the NOx Protocol seemed to them to have come out of the blue. DOE was already on the defensive internationally, but now it was being bombarded with criticism domestically. At the same time, DOE negotiators believed that the NOx Protocol would not adversely affect the primary energy industry.

Oil and gas interests were, however, extremely angry at the lack of consultation and at the longer-term commitments to the reduction of emissions that the NOx Protocol implied. While they went after DOE directly, their preferred arena for lobbying was the Department of External Affairs. In several closed meetings with then Minister for External Affairs Joe Clark and his officials, the Alberta energy lobby criticized department officials for having let such a situation arise. This was one of several such controversies that prompted External Affairs to attempt to reassert its primacy in environmental foreign policy.

The pattern and nature of business criticism was also affected by the decision of the Canadian Council of Ministers of the Environment to launch a massive stakeholder exercise to develop a management plan for the control of NOx and VOCs. At one stroke, the business interests involved were expanded well beyond those in the energy sector to include groups as disparate as drycleaners and perfume manufacturers.[16] Combining VOCs with NOx made sense not only because the hazards were interdependent but also because VOCs were already the subject of negotiations on a separate protocol.

The provinces had been almost as vociferous in their criticism of DOE as elements of the business community had been. Their concerns were partly jurisdictional, but they also arose because NOx-VOCs emissions were not a serious problem in some parts of the country. Hence, given scarce environmental time and resources, some provinces preferred to put their money and priorities elsewhere. Nonetheless, an elaborate NOx-VOCs management process

---

16 See Doern, "Regulation and Incentives," pp. 101–107.

was launched that became, in effect, a post-protocol consultation process on NOx and a pre-protocol consultation process on VOCs. A VOCs Protocol was signed in 1991.

Neither business nor the ENGOs could be said to have been at the table during the NOx Protocol negotiations. For its part, External Affairs was clearly unhappy with how the NOx issue had been handled, while DOE saw the NOx Protocol process, at least with hindsight, as something to avoid in the future. Some of the significant process problems were, in DOE's view, based on rhetorical excess by energy interests campaigning against not only the NOx process but also, by 1990, against the larger Green Plan, which many were beginning to equate with the infamous National Energy Program of 1980. In some quarters, at least, the whole process of environmental policy reform was seen as an unfriendly intervention by Eastern Canada against Western Canadian interests. (Appendix 2 summarizes the main events surrounding the decisionmaking processes on LRTAP, SO_2, and NOx.)

The Ozone Convention and the Montreal Protocol

Occurring halfway through the 1980s, but eventually overlapping with the LRTAP-SO_2-NOx story, was the decisionmaking process leading to the 1985 Vienna Convention for the Protection of the Ozone Layer and the subsequent adoption of the 1987 Montreal Protocol on Substances that Deplete the Ozone Layer and its further amendment in 1990.[17]

The key international agency involved was the United Nations Environmental Programme (UNEP). The Vienna Convention signa-

---

17 See E.P. Barratt-Brown, "Building a Monitoring and Compliance Regime under the Montreal Protocol," *Yale Journal of International Law* 16 (1990): 520–570; W. Lang, "From Vienna to Montreal and Beyond: The Politics of Ozone Layer Protection" (Vienna, 1989, Mimeographed); and G.V. Buxton, "UNCED and Lessons from the Montreal Protocol," *Law and Contemporary Problems* (forthcoming, 1992).

tories could not agree in 1985 on any kind of detailed control program so the convention was very much a framework document providing for international monitoring and scientific assessment activities. Importantly, however, it did establish a firm commitment to adopt a control protocol within a two-year period.

The Montreal Protocol provided for an initial set of targets for reducing the production and consumption of ozone-depleting chemicals. It also set up a detailed process for periodic scientific review leading to further changes to the targets. These revised targets would take into account the availability of substitutes, environmental impacts, and the economics of different control options.[18] The protocol aimed to reduce the consumption of chlorofluorocarbons in the late 1990s to 50 percent of 1986 levels and to freeze the consumption of halons in 1992 at 1986 levels. The 1990 London revisions, which occurred after new research showed even more serious environmental effects, committed the signatories to reduce CFCs to 50 percent of 1986 levels by 1995 with an eventual phaseout entirely by 2000. Halons would follow a roughly similar pattern.

For Canada, the stratospheric ozone issue was quite different from its earlier experience with SO_2 and NOx. Not only were many more countries involved in a truly global hazard, but Canada's direct contribution to the problem was quite small, barely 2 percent of world production. At the same time, Canada's CFC and halon-producing industries and those consuming such products were by no means trivial parts of this country's economy. In the main, however, Canada was free to play the role of a helpful fixer and mediator on the international stage.

The journey to the Montreal Protocol started with the publication of scientific research in 1974, warning of the strong possibility of ozone-layer depletion by manmade chemicals such as CFCs. CFCs are used as solvents in thousands of products, including aerosol cans, refrigeration, transportation, and plastics. Used with halons,

---

18 See R.E. Benedick, *Ozone Diplomacy: New Directions in Safeguarding the Planet* (Cambridge, Mass.: Harvard University Press, 1991).

they are also a key component of fire extinguishers. Because of their stable chemical structure, CFCs can remain in the atmosphere for many decades or even centuries. Thus, even if production and use stopped immediately, there would be long-term adverse effects on the ozone layer, which is key to protecting the earth from the sun's ultraviolet rays.

Canada's initial response to the ozone issue occurred in 1978, when regulations were approved to ban the use of aerosol sprays.[19] Generally, however, the international reaction was sluggish. The CFC industry responded almost immediately by challenging the research and calling for more study.

UNEP, for its part, saw ozone depletion as a potentially serious issue. As early as 1977, it set up a Coordinating Committee on the Ozone Layer and urged a worldwide action plan. By 1981, some basic agreement had been reached on the scientific issues involved — which is one of the most important prerequisites for protocol making.[20] In 1982, UNEP established a working group of legal and technical experts to develop the outlines of a framework convention and to mobilize support from a coalition of states, agencies, and ENGOs. After three years, however, the working group was unable to marshal a coalition of supporters, for several reasons that struck at the core of the international political economy of the CFC industry.

First, there was still sufficient scientific uncertainty and controversy about the processes driving ozone depletion to give key interests an excuse to stall. Second, the Reagan Administration was simply not interested in giving environmental issues much of a priority. The United States did join Canada and the Nordic countries in pressing for the inclusion of an international ban on aerosols in

---

19 See G.B. Doern, *Regulatory and Jurisdictional Issues in the Regulation of Hazardous Substances in Canada* (Ottawa: Science Council of Canada, 1977).

20 Agreement on the scientific issues does not necessarily mean unanimity but, rather, increasing agreement within a band of probabilities — what is sometimes called "the politics of hypotheticality." See G.B. Doern, *The Peripheral Nature of Scientific Controversy in Federal Policy Formation* (Ottawa: Science Council of Canada, 1981).

the convention, but it was unprepared to lead the issue. Instead, Washington had its eye fixed firmly on the posture being developed by the European Community.

At that time, EC countries had about 45 percent of the world CFC market, about one-third of it exported to developing countries, which were not then key players in the negotiation process.[21] Dominant firms such as ICI in Britain and Atochem in France had tremendous clout with EC negotiators and feared losing their world market share to US producers during any phaseout period. The US industry, having already phased out aerosols, simply was better technologically prepared to offer product substitutes. Thus, for most of the 1982–85 period, the United States and the EC, backed by their industry lobbies, checkmated each other.

Some counterpressure emerged from the ENGOs, mainly through court action in the United States.[22] A lawsuit brought in 1984 by the Natural Resources Defense Council led to a court order requiring the US Environmental Protection Agency to develop domestic regulations for CFCs by 1987 or to explain why it had not done so. This led to further cooperative action between the agency and UNEP, including a US proposal that CFCs be phased out by the turn of the century.

There was thus sufficient political will by 1985 for 32 countries to adopt the Vienna Convention, but strong opposition from EC producers meant that there would still be no control program. The convention did, however, create further momentum for progress, including the commitment to have an agreed protocol within two years. UNEP immediately established two workshops, on scientific data and on control options and regimes, with members drawn from the UN, Third World and developed country officials, the ENGOs, business, and academia; there were no official national delegates. The workshop on control options and regimes met in a rural, infor-

---

21 The United States accounted for 30 percent of world production, Japan and the USSR about 10 percent each, and the rest was spread among a few other developed states, including Canada.

22 See Barratt-Brown, "Building a Monitoring and Compliance Regime," pp. 532–542.

mal setting at Leesburg, Virginia, near Washington, and it was here that US ENGOs arguably first became directly involved in international negotiations.

By this time, considerable policy entrepreneurial zeal was being offered to move the process forward. It came from three main sources: the Executive Director of UNEP, Mostafa Tolba; the United States, which had taken the lead on the scientific work, much of which was now being run through the National Aeronautics and Space Administration; and Canada, which had suggested control options.[23] Canada's leadership role in the protocol process culminated in the decision to hold negotiations in Montreal. The negotiations were difficult, lasted several tense days, and were resolved only in the last few hours.

The Montreal Protocol was designed to enable as many countries as possible to sign. Within the framework of phased reductions, therefore, countries were given considerable flexibility in reaching their lower emission limits.[24] The control package also sought to ensure that reductions occurred first in developed states. Here, control centered on consumption, with a formula devised to include export and import totals. This, it was hoped, would forge a consensus between the EC and the United States.[25] The control regime was also meant to ensure that an increase in production and consumption did not occur in Third World countries. For example, the agreement provided that developed countries could not produce more than 10 percent over their domestic consumption quota for export to developing countries. As a further inducement, Third World coun-

23 See G.V. Buxton, A. Chisolm and J. Carbonneau, "A Canadian Contribution to the Consideration of Strategies for Protecting the Ozone Layer" (Paper presented at the UNEP Workshop on Economic Issues Related to Control of CFCs, Leesburg, Virginia, September 8–12, 1986).

24 See D.A. Smith, "The Implementation of Policies to Protect the Ozone Layer," in Doern, ed., *Getting It Green*, pp. 111–128.

25 See A. Enders and A. Porges, "Successful Conventions and Conventional Success: Saving the Ozone Layer," in K. Anderson and R. Blackhurst, eds., *The Greening of World Trade Issues* (London: Harvester Wheatsheaf, 1992), pp. 130–144.

tries with a low per capita use of CFCs were granted a ten-year delay in meeting the reduced emission targets. These countries were also promised financial help to ensure that they incurred no net new costs, as well as assistance with new technologies.

The ink was barely dry on the Montreal Protocol when stunning new research in 1988 revealed the existence of a huge hole in the ozone layer over Antarctica. This was followed almost immediately by an announcement by Du Pont, by far the largest CFC producer, that it would phase out production of all CFCs and halons by 2000 and would invest heavily in the development of product substitutes. Occurring as they did in the midst of the global warming scare exacerbated by an unusually hot summer, these findings escalated international environmental lobbying by a remarkably broad coalition of over 90 ENGOs from 27 countries.

Scientific pressure and lobbying by the ENGOs eventually led the signatory countries of the Montreal Protocol to meet in London in June 1990. By convening the meeting, Britain hoped to protect markets in developing countries for key domestic producers, such as ICI, and to improve the Thatcher government's environmental image. The meeting's chief accomplishments, however, were twofold. First, an International Technology Review Panel was set up to determine the technical feasibility of toughening the emission-reduction targets established by the Montreal Protocol. The panel reported that it was indeed possible to do so, and the London meeting produced amendments strengthening the Protocol. Second, another panel, charged with developing a funding mechanism, succeeded in getting the signatories to establish a multilateral fund to help developing countries meet their reduction targets. Since the availability of money would be conditional on meeting targets, the fund would also act as a compliance mechanism.

Appendix 3 summarizes the chronology of events leading to the signing of the Ozone Convention and the Montreal Protocol, and subsequent amendments. It is appropriate at this stage to take a closer look at the interplay of key Canadian interests in the larger international decisionmaking process.

The Role of Canadian ENGOs

Canadian ENGOs had been involved in the mid- and late 1970s in pressing for a ban on aerosols. But when larger CFC issues emerged in the mid-1980s, their role was a mixed and somewhat limited one. In part, this was due to their limited technical knowledge on CFCs. DOE did brief groups such as Friends of the Earth on the state of play of the 1985 negotiations, but the ENGOs' goal was a simplistic one of achieving the deepest cuts possible.

DOE organized a further briefing and discussion session on the Montreal Protocol in August 1987, but only eight people turned up, and none from ENGOs. Nonetheless, through coordination with Friends of the Earth International, one ENGO representative became a member of the Canadian delegation. The environment minister and key officials could not suppress their anger, however, when this representative publicly criticized Canada's role in not pressing for deeper cuts.

In general, then, Canada's ENGOs were not the key players in the ozone story that they had been in the overall SO_2 dynamics. Rather, the most consistent international pressure was exerted by large and expert US ENGOs such as the Environmental Defense Fund and the World Resources Institute. And US ENGOs were largely responsible for putting together the impressive coalition of ENGOs referred to earlier.

The Role of Canadian Business

Canadian business interests had an important, but not pivotal, role in the overall international scheme of things. The main players, Du Pont Canada and Allied Chemical,[26] tended to echo the larger global tactics of their US parents and, in the mid-1980s, fought the effort to impose a controls program. But as early as September 1986,

---

26 Another key firm was C-I-L Inc. Unlike the other two firms, which were large producers of CFCs, C-I-L's involvement was as an importer of CFC-related materials.

Du Pont Canada began to argue that there should be a capping program, which angered its industrial competitors who had hoped to maintain a united front. Allied Chemical, for example, was not doing nearly as much R&D work on technological substitutes and hence knew that it was vulnerable. When Du Pont Canada's US parent announced it was getting out of CFCs, the dykes broke both domestically and internationally. Thereafter, the firms' concerns centered on ensuring that the Montreal Protocol control program had the necessary flexibility.

Conclusions

The experience with two major international environmental conventions and three protocols during the 1980s offers a dynamic insight into the substance of the deals and the domestic and international processes involved in reaching international environmental agreements. For each of the players, the dynamics varied with the different physical realities of the hazard. Each of the players also had to find a way to deal with the new environmental political economy that was increasingly in evidence.

The role of science was crucial at the earlier stages and in launching later reviews. Science was also becoming gradually more institutionalized, rather than freelance, in that it was built into the very framework of conventions and protocols. Good science was an essential prerequisite, a point brought home to DOE by its confidence in handling the SO_2 case and its uncertainty in the NOx case.

The ENGOs' involvement was muted, first in the LRTAP-SO_2 case — where the international arena was relegated almost to a sideshow while attention focused on the bilateral Canada-US arena — then in the ozone case, where Canadian ENGOs found themselves inadequately prepared to make an effective contribution. Internationally, however, a considerable coalition of ENGOs was mobilized, mainly by organizations from the United States.

Business interests initially offered strong resistance to international regulatory pressures, but eventually collaborated. The change in strategy was often triggered by key, technologically advanced firms deciding that they could prosper by using product substitutes. They sometimes had better access to international negotiators than did the ENGOs, but were angered at times by the failure to include them in the consultative process — as was the case during negotiations on the NOx Protocol. By the end of the 1980s, business was pressing hard for a more institutionalized process. On balance, however, the process was a successful one. An independent assessment of the Montreal Protocol praised the inclusion and active involvement of private sector organizations, such as business, labor, and independent scientists, in the meetings and negotiations. The study concluded that progress "might not have been possible without the participation of industry and environmental groups."[27]

---

27 See W.A. Nitze, *The Greenhouse Effect: Formulating a Convention* (London: Royal Institute of International Affairs, 1990), p. 23.

Chapter 4

Consensus and Conflict in the 1990s: The Road to Rio

This chapter provides an analytical bridge between the 1980s and the early 1990s by looking briefly at more recent developments in the dynamics of reaching international environmental agreements. The analysis is more illustrative because most of the decisionmaking processes — such as the giant 1992 United Nations Conference on Environment and Development (UNCED) in Rio de Janeiro, the "Rio Earth Summit" — are very recent. The array of cases covered in this chapter — the Basle Convention, the Bergen meetings, the climate change negotiations, and the Rio Earth Summit — especially reflects the fact that the environmental agenda of the early 1990s is unambiguously global, involving many interactive pollutants and substances, and fiercely complex.[1]

The chapter begins with a look at two international events that span the two decades and reveal further growing pains in the decisionmaking process: the 1989 Basle Convention on the Control of Transboundary Movements of Hazardous Wastes, and the 1988–90 process leading to the Bergen meetings of May 1990. The chapter then examines the early dynamics of preparing for the Rio Earth Summit in 1992, including its work on biodiversity and forestry agreements. The third part of the chapter examines the related early

---

1 See J.T. Mathews, "Redefining Security," *Foreign Affairs* 68 (Spring 1989): 162–177; and F.O. Hampson, "New Wine in Old Bottles: The International Politics of the Environment" (Paper presented to the Conference on the New World Situation and the Future of Peace, Hobart and William Smith Colleges, Geneva, New York, April, 27, 1991).

dynamics regarding the negotiation of a convention on climate change. The chapter concludes by looking at how these events and pressures have redefined the core relationship between the Department of the Environment (DOE) and the Department of External Affairs and International Trade (EAITC).

From Basle to Bergen: More Growing Pains

In 1988, an Italian ship was discovered dumping hazardous wastes off the coast of Nigeria. Incidents of this kind had happened before, of course, but the media coverage of this one was sufficient to spur the United Nations Environmental Programme, led by Mostafa Tolba, into action.

The resulting convention signed at Basle, Switzerland, in 1989 seemed at first glance to be a fairly innocuous framework agreement, basically setting up a notification and information process.[2] The convention also contained an annex listing various hazardous substances, which did not sufficiently differentiate between wastes that were being destroyed from those that were being recycled. Environmentally, the latter were, of course, to be encouraged and the former discouraged. Canada signed the convention but delayed ratification pending the development of a special fast-track process for recycled wastes.

In some respects, the Basle Convention case was similar to the nitrogen oxide (NOx) case examined in Chapter 3 in that it was a group of aggrieved domestic industry interests — the Canadian Mining Association and assertive firms such as IPSCO in Regina — that rang the alarm bells. They attacked what they saw as "lone ranger"-style protocol setting, lobbied EAITC fiercely, and took a strip off DOE both directly and through other ministers and members of Parliament in Ottawa.

---

2 See United Nations Environmental Programme, *Basle Convention on the Control of Transboundary Movements of Hazardous Wastes*, Basle, Switzerland, March 22, 1989.

In contrast to the NOx case, however, DOE officials felt that the rhetorical anger of the criticism was unwarranted. This was again because of the genuinely difficult technical problems in differentiating between materials that were to undergo destruction and those that were to be recycled. Nonetheless, Basle was also lumped with NOx in DOE's list of examples of how not to develop international agreements.

The combined effects of the Basle and NOx cases and the impending negotiations on climate change also prompted EAITC's environment sector to propose ways in which EAITC could strengthen its capacity to influence foreign policy and the environment. The proposals centered on three areas that seemed to be within EAITC's mandate: improving the transparency of information for domestic interest groups, especially business; clarifying environment-trade policy issues; and promoting trade in environmental products.

On the first of these items, EAITC's environment group ventured the idea of holding regular meetings with business and other interests. This led to a heated turf battle with DOE, which, led by powerful Minister of the Environment Lucien Bouchard, was just gearing up for its massive 1990 Green Plan.[3] In any event, the idea for business consultation did not go forward but became a part of the later melding of processes proposed in the Green Plan. Another stream of consciousness feeding into these later processes was the Bergen exercise.

The meetings held in Bergen, Norway, May 8–16, 1990, were planned as a follow-up on the Brundtland Report of 1987,[4] which

---

3 Canada, *Canada's Green Plan* (Ottawa: Supply and Services Canada, 1990). For critiques, see G.B. Doern, *Shades of Green: Gauging Canada's Green Plan*, C.D. Howe Institute Commentary 29 (Toronto: C.D. Howe Institute, 1991); and G. Toner, "Passionate Politics: Canada's Green Plan for Social Change," *Ecodecision* 1 (Spring 1991).

4 See World Commission on Environment and Development, *Our Common Future*, chaired by Norwegian Prime Minister Gro Harlem Brundtland (Oxford: Oxford University Press, 1987); and Regional Conference on the Follow-up to the World Commission on Environment and Development in the ECE Region, *Action for a Common Future* (Bergen, Norway, May 8–16, 1990).

had recommended that conferences be held on national, regional, and global levels to develop measures to institutionalize the concept of sustainable development that it had championed. The United Nations Economic Commission for Europe (ECE) had, as a result, agreed to sponsor the Bergen Conference for the ECE region.

The particular aim of the Bergen Conference was to build on the Brundtland Report's theme of fostering partnerships among all levels of society. Accordingly, the processes for preparing an action plan to emanate from the conference involved extensive input from government, business, environmental nongovernmental organizations (ENGOs), labor unions, scientists, and youth. Canada had been a particularly strong supporter of the Brundtland Report's approach and had launched its own environment-economy task force as well as an array of environmental roundtables.

The Bergen Conference was expected to produce two significant results: a Joint Agenda for Action for which all sectors would be equally accountable, and a Ministerial Statement on Sustainable Development in the ECE Region. Initial consultations led to the development of four main agenda items: awareness raising and public participation, sustainable industrial activity, sustainable energy use, and the economics of sustainability.

Because the essence of the conference was to stimulate cross-sectoral dialogue and foster alliance building — and to do so on a massive international scale — the exercise was greeted with considerable skepticism by many environmental and foreign affairs ministries among the ECE states. Nonetheless, considerable preparatory work went into the exercise. In late 1989 and early 1990, four workshops on the selected themes were held in four different countries. These groups were multisectoral in composition and reviewed progress in the various countries in implementing the Brundtland Report's recommendations.

The international ENGOs engaged in their own separate preparations for the Bergen Conference, with representatives of more than 300 of them meeting in March 1990 on the Danube. An industry forum organized through the International Chamber of Commerce brought together about 200 chief executive officers of corporations from 25 countries. Similar sessions were held for youth, scientists, and trade unions. Each preparatory session produced its proposals for the eventual joint action agenda.

The Bergen Conference itself consisted of an initial working session followed by a ministerial session. The working session was attended by 427 delegates, including 173 from ENGOs. Each theme was discussed in open forum, but the negotiations were limited to governmental and ENGO representatives. The conference was one of the first international exercises bringing together such a diverse set of players. Inevitably, therefore, the Joint Agenda for Action and the Ministerial Statement on Sustainable Development tended to be little more than general statements of good intentions and elaborate wish lists, but many still judged the Bergen experience to have been successful in breaking new environmental ground, particularly with regard to the international participation of business and the ENGOs.

Alas, the conference also showed the pitfalls of the international agreement process. Originally, the conference had been the initiative of then Norwegian Prime Minister Gro Harlem Brundtland, who, no doubt, would have been satisfied with receiving credit simply for the multisector approach that was used. By the time the conference was held, however, the Brundtland government had been replaced by a more conservative regime looking for something a little less broad and a lot more concrete to promote its environmental credentials at home and abroad. It wanted Bergen to be remembered as an event at which some decisive steps were taken on the burgeoning issue of global warming. Above all, the dynamics involved ensured that the host nation and its allies could paint other countries, especially the United States, as the international laggards.

Tactical media environmental one-upmanship was the order of the day at the conference. A US telex to its own embassies was leaked — by the Americans themselves, some suspected, to avoid the United States' being isolated as the environmental villain — saying that Canada, Britain, and the USSR were planning to form an alliance at the conference to block a group of European countries that wanted to move quickly to fight global warming. At a meeting in Holland the previous November, the United States, Japan, and Britain had moved to make sure specific targets for carbon dioxide emissions were not set for industrial nations. At that meeting, Canada had aligned with the Nordic countries, which were looking for a stronger set of rules. At the Bergen Conference, Norway, West Germany, Belgium, France, Denmark, Sweden, and Holland were expected to push for a freeze on carbon dioxide emissions at present levels by the end of the decade.

Canada's delegation at Bergen was headed by DOE rather than by EAITC. It was caught off guard by the US leak and was insufficiently warned of the changing tactics of the Norwegian government in going for a global warming ministerial focus.

In response, Canada's fiercely independent Minister of the Environment, Lucien Bouchard, issued a statement that others back in Ottawa, including EAITC officials, regarded as premature at best and difficult actually to implement at worst. Bouchard issued a separate verbal promise, separate from the common position of the 34 countries, that Canada's carbon dioxide emissions would be no higher in 2000 than they were at the time of the conference. Environment ministers from a few other countries also made similar stronger separate public commitments.

Bouchard's statement aroused considerable anger among Canadian energy interests, becoming almost immediately ensnared in the larger politics surrounding the federal Green Plan, which Bouchard was heading. Energy and political interests in Western Canada were already labeling the prospective Green Plan and its feared potential carbon taxes as another interventionist and divisive equivalent of the National Energy Program. Bouchard resigned over the constitutional crisis almost immediately after the Bergen Conference, but steps were already being taken to ensure that energetic environment ministers did not make foreign environmental policy that was too far ahead of the domestic consensus.

As for the larger process, DOE officials regarded the Bergen experiment as well worth the effort. From the outset, DOE felt that it could offer its own considerable experience with institutional change. Its experience with multisector stakeholder processes, round-tables, and other reforms was quite advanced by international standards. DOE tried to facilitate the involvement of Canadian ENGOs, business, youth, unions, and scientists in the Bergen process. It found its own processes to be quite collegial almost to the end, until the politics of global warming took hold in Bergen. At this point, Canada's ENGO participants joined their fellow international ENGOs in lambasting their home country's record. Once again, DOE officials were disappointed and frustrated with some Canadian ENGOs because they regarded these tactics as a violation of the entire spirit of Bergen and of the leadup process.

The internal Canadian process also exhibited some important practical problems. First, there was the usual difficulty of finding appropriate representatives, particularly for the youth delegation — although these problems eventually were solved. Second, much of the consultation and exchange among the groups was through papers rather than face-to-face contact. Third, the Canadians never met as a delegation prior to going to Bergen, partly because of the difficulty of fitting a meeting into the schedules of a group of very busy people. With DOE's support, however, many Canadian non-governmental participants were extremely active in the Bergen sessions. Fourth, the consultation process also involved other federal departments such as Finance and Energy, Mines and Resources to complement the DOE-led preparatory process.

The Bergen Conference raised concerns about just how cohesive and trustful delegations can become when composed of multisector representatives, as Canada's clearly was. It must be remembered, however, that the conference was not initially seen as a negotiating forum in the sense that protocol-setting sessions are.

The Rio Earth Summit Process and the Consultation Maze

The lessons of Bergen were barely being digested when the Rio Earth Summit process began. Indeed, for the United Nations, Bergen was simply a preparatory conference for the larger UNCED meeting scheduled for Brazil in June 1992. UN Resolution 44/228, passed in December 1989, set out the broad and ambitious purposes of the massive Rio de Janeiro meetings.[5] More than 30,000 people attended the June 1992 meetings, including about 22,000 from ENGOs, and women's, youth, and labor groups. Again, as at Bergen, a multisector approach to the process and substance of the meetings was the hallmark of the Rio Summit.

The Summit achieved several concrete things, in addition to drawing unprecedented media attention to the serious degradation of the world's life-support systems.[6] First, an impressive group of world political leaders signed the Rio Declaration, which sets out, among other principles, the need for public participation, environmental precautionary measures, and affirmation of the notion that the "polluter must pay." Canada and some other countries had hoped to see a more ambitious "Earth Charter" develop; in the event, Prime Minister Brian Mulroney became the first world leader to endorse the negotiation of a full Earth Charter by 1995.

A second achievement at Rio was the endorsement of Agenda 21, an action plan for the twenty-first century. Agenda 21 is a massive, 500-page document with 40 chapters of environmental and economic proposals on promoting sustainable development through trade; combating poverty; human settlements; the role of women; indigenous peoples; the integration of the environment and the economy in decisionmaking; the oceans; freshwater; toxic chemicals; hazardous wastes; and radioactive wastes.[7]

A third achievement was the signing of the Biodiversity Convention. Though media attention focused on the refusal of the United

---

5 See G.V. Buxton, "UNCED and Lessons from the Montreal Protocol," *Law and Contemporary Problems* (forthcoming, 1992); and J. MacNeill and R. Munro, "Environment 1972–1992: From the Margin to the Mainstream," *Ecodecision* 1 (Spring 1991): 19–23.

6 See Canada, Department of the Environment, "Earth Summit Summary Assessment," *Press Release*, August 1992.

7 Ibid, pp. 2–7.

States to sign, the convention was nonetheless significant. Its signatories committed themselves to protect endangered species and the
areas they inhabit. National biodiversity strategies are to be developed, along with commitments from developed countries to provide
developing countries with funds, technologies, and related assistance for conservation measures. The convention also sets rules
whereby tropical countries will make their plants and animals available to developed countries for genetic experimentation on the
condition that they share in the profits derived from any resulting
commercial products.

Finally, Rio saw the signing of a declaration of principles on
forests.[8] A convention on forests was a major Canadian goal at
UNCED, but very early in the negotiations it was apparent that
developing countries with forest resources — such as Malaysia and
India — opposed a convention that would contain concrete commitments. It is also unlikely that there was sufficient federal-provincial
agreement within Canada, a fact that was not seriously tested when
it was apparent that international agreement was unlikely.

The UNCED decisionmaking process was both bewilderingly
complex and unprecedented in its magnitude and the degree of
involvement by various sectoral groups and governments. It is
difficult to know what criteria one could use to assess whether
Canada's overall consensus formation processes for Rio were successful or not. The vastness of the agenda and its applicable time
frame into the next century, the complexity of the necessary coalition
building both within national delegations and among the delegations of other countries, and the mixture of exhilaration and fatigue
felt by many Canadian business and ENGO participants make judg-
ment difficult.

The overall UNCED process involved two phases. The first
phase was the development, over two years and through four massive meetings of the Preparatory Committees, of Agenda 21, the

---

8 The successful negotiation prior to the Earth Summit of the United Nations
 Framework Convention on Climate Change, which is examined in more detail
 below, was also signed at Rio.

Earth Charter (later the Rio Declaration), and the Convention on Forests. Separate preparatory meetings were also being held by representatives from business, youth, women, and environmental groups. Meanwhile, in separate intergovernmental groups, the conventions on climate change and biodiversity were being negotiated. The second phase involved the two-week Rio Earth Summit itself, where there was considerable fine tuning and last-minute bargaining over issues that had been postponed until the political leaders became engaged.

Canada's input into the Preparatory Committees, and hence into the Agenda 21 and Earth Charter processes, was multisectoral and multidepartmental — more or less in line with the Bergen model, but with the important addition of the separate sectoral group meetings. DOE anchored the process, but the Canadian delegation was headed by EAITC. ENGO and business involvement was extensive, but these processes were largely devoted to negotiating and fighting for various items in an agenda or for various kinds of principles in a charter — they were not negotiations about concrete targets and control mechanisms. Thus, both DOE and the various groups expressed satisfaction or dissatisfaction according to whether or not their key concepts or paragraphs found their way into the agreed text of Agenda 21.

At Rio itself, especially given the unprecedented media exposure of global green issues and the positions of political leaders, the process was part circus and part slogging backroom work and drafting. The Canadian positions and interpretations of success and failure must be seen against the backdrop of the larger canvas of world environmental politics prior to and at Rio. At the center of this were the tactics and positions of the United States.

US President George Bush had used his participation in the Rio Earth Summit as a bargaining chip in the negotiations on the Convention on Climate Change, saying that he would not attend if the convention contained specific targets and commitments. This stance worked. The convention, as we see below, was agreed to before President Bush showed up in Rio to sign it. At Rio itself, the United

States refused to sign the Convention on Biodiversity, but pushed hard on the need for solid forestry agreements. Its hardball negotiating stance and disappointing lack of leadership earned it a deserved low ranking in the world ENGO and press scorecards at Rio. Even William Reilly, head of the Environmental Protection Agency, criticized his political masters for playing a "low key defensive game."[9] One must look beyond these judgments, however, to see the cascading effects of the United States' position on other negotiating tactics and then on how domestic Canadian interests might view their role or that of their government in the process as a whole.

The fact that the United States was prepared to play the role of environmental villain — at least publicly — meant that other countries did not have to deal with economic realities in a severe, anti-environmental way. The United States mishandled the public relations aspects of its international environmental diplomacy badly, but, in fact, the US record in many environmental areas is vastly superior to that of the European Community (EC), which itself was quite divided over environmental issues — so much so that its Environment Commissioner, Carlo Ripa di Meana, resigned prior to Rio, dismissing the Summit as the "high school of hypocrisy" and arguing that the EC had "nothing to offer in Rio."[10]

During the two-week Rio process, the ENGOs kept up pressure on world leaders in a variety of ways. In one media event, for example, four groups — Greenpeace, Friends of the Earth, Third World Network, and the Forum of Brazilian NGOs — challenged the US, the EC, and Japanese delegations to meet them to discuss a ten-point plan to "save the Earth Summit."[11] The groups issued their challenge in front of 300 journalists against the backdrop of a poverty-stricken Rio shanty town, Rocinha. Another set of groups issued a Summit report card that ranked the United States, Saudi Arabia, and Britain as the worst performers at Rio; Canada got a quite good

---

9 Quoted in *Washington Post*, August 2, 1992, p. 2.
10 Quoted in *The Independent* (London), June 14, 1992, p. 8.
11 *The Independent* (London), June 8, 1992, p. 13.

grade.[12] On the other hand, just prior to Rio, unnamed "excessive" environmental groups were themselves chastized in a declaration addressed to world leaders and signed by more than 200 scientists and intellectuals, including 54 Nobel Prize winners, which expressed concern at the emergence of an "irrational ideology which is opposed to scientific and industrial progress and impedes economic and social development."[13]

Canadian positions also cannot be divorced from these larger lobbying realities. For example, although DOE genuinely wanted a convention on climate change with control mechanisms and targets built in, other parts of the government, along with some provincial and private energy interests, breathed a sigh of relief when the United States did their negotiating for them and took the political flak to boot. The relief is likely to be brief, however, since Prime Minister Mulroney committed Canada to tough action regardless of whether or not the convention contained control measures.

None of this is intended to argue that Canada's delegates did not show negotiating leadership in many areas. Indeed, Canada seems genuinely to have done well and to have earned respect at Rio, but this complex series of processes allowed Canada, at least to some extent, a free ride on the back of the hardball strategy of the United States. Other Canadian domestic players also inevitably began to see the process differently when negotiations became more complex. Now, though they may still cling to their core positions and preferences, the more they are part of an unwieldy and complicated global process and the more they see and experience it first hand, the more they appreciate the practical dilemmas their own government faces.

Indeed, it is appropriate at this stage of the analysis to speak of environmental policymakers and sectoral participants alike as increasingly having to function, in UNCED-style processes, in a kind of consultation maze. All parties demand to participate, but when they do they find themselves in a labyrinth. All participants want to keep all their options open as to which arenas of consultation and

---

12 *The Independent* (London), June 11, 1992, p. 11.

13 *The Independent*, June 1, 1992, p. 1.

power to use to their own advantage, but all of them long for simple, one-stop policy shopping.

Moreover, by the time of the UNCED process, consultation was no longer occurring at the somewhat more leisurely rate of the early 1980s, when it seemed possible to deal with one hazard every five years or so. By 1990, both the international environmental agenda and the domestic agenda were making numerous concurrent demands, often on the same interest groups involved and often on the same key players in those groups. For example, the environmental consultations calendar prepared periodically by the Non-Governmental Relations Division of DOE showed in 1991 that the department was then engaged in over 70 consultative exercises.[14] This list did not include several anticipated major Green Plan issues or talks related to UNCED. In addition, other federal departments were engaged in their own consultative exercises with some of the same interests to obtain parallel views that would feed into their rivalries with DOE — including, of course, positions on international agreements and protocols. Inevitably, many of these exercises overlapped in a way that the groups involved sometimes regarded as disorganized.

This frustration spawned a number of reform efforts. EAITC's initial effort to design a consultative and early warning system for business has already been noted, but other mechanisms were being fostered as well. First, by 1990, Environmental Roundtables — permanent, multisector advisory and consultative bodies operating at the federal and provincial levels — were active and working. Second, the Canadian Environmental Network, the Canadian ENGOs' main umbrella body, formed its own international affairs caucus. Third, key business groups and DOE got together to form the Friday Group, consisting of several knowledgeable industrial people who, on their own initiative or at DOE's request, could offer advice and feedback on pending issues and topics dealing with the environment and business. And fourth, in the federal-provincial arena, steps were

---

14 See Canada, Department of the Environment, Non-Governmental Relations Division, "Environmental Consultations Calendar," Ottawa, July 1991.

taken to ensure that, as much as possible, the Canadian Council of Ministers of the Environment became the main forum for consultation on international issues, including UNCED and its aftermath.

The Domestic Decisionmaking Process for a Climate Change Convention

The United Nations Framework Convention on Climate Change, although signed at Rio, was negotiated before the Rio meetings and through a separate process. To contrast the necessarily unwieldy UNCED process, it is useful to look briefly at the decisionmaking process that led to the more specific Climate Change Convention.

While aspects of global warming had been studied for some time, The issue was firmly placed on the international agenda by major scientific conferences held in Villach, Austria, in 1984 and Bellagio, Italy, in 1987.[15] The early stages of the process remained a largely scientific matter filled with massive uncertainty.[16] As a result, the United Nations Environmental Programme and the World Meteorological Organization jointly decided in 1988 to establish an Intergovernmental Panel on Climate Change (IPCC). Canadian leadership also led to a World Conference on the Changing Atmosphere in Toronto in the summer of 1988. The heat waves and drought conditions that characterized that summer gave the issue a political and mass media impetus of unexpected proportions.

The IPCC established three working groups that, though centered on scientific concerns, increasingly involved sensitive political and policy issues as well. The first group, chaired by Britain, dealt with the science of global warming. The second group, on the impacts of global warming, was headed by the Soviet Union. The United States chaired the third group, on policy responses to global

---

15 See J. Jaeger et al., *Developing Policies for Responding to Climate Change* (Stockholm: Beijer Institute and World Meteorological Organization, April 1988).

16 See K. Hare, "Environmental Uncertainty: Science and the Greenhouse Effect," in G.B. Doern, ed., *The Environmental Imperative: Market Approaches to the Greening of Canada* (Toronto: C.D. Howe Institute, 1990), pp. 19–34.

warming, which became the battleground for key political concerns. During this period, a Ministerial Conference held in Noordwijk, Holland, in November 1989 provided further political momentum with the release of a declaration in which the major industrialized countries committed to stabilize greenhouse gas emissions as soon as possible. The reports of the three IPCC working groups were finalized in August 1990 and fed into the Second World Climate Conference, held in Geneva in November 1990. At this conference, governments expressed broad agreement with the findings of the IPCC report and launched a formal negotiation process for a convention on climate change.

At the earlier 1989 Noordwijk meeting, the EC, Canada, Australia, and New Zealand had sought to obtain a commitment to stabilize carbon dioxide (CO_2) emissions by the year 2000 but the United States, Japan, and the Soviet Union had refused. Later, at the Bergen Conference in May 1990, Britain committed itself to stabilizing CO_2 emissions at 1990 levels by 2005, provided that other countries were prepared to bear their share of the problem. As we saw earlier, Bergen was also an arena for attempting to push as many countries as possible into specific target commitments, especially on CO_2 emissions.

At the Economic Summit of the Group of Seven in Houston in July 1990, it was agreed that a climate convention should be negotiated by the end of 1992, the upcoming June 1992 Rio Earth Summit providing further impetus for this timetable. By the time the negotiations began in 1991, there was also considerable consensus about what would have to be in a convention on global warming.[17] First, there would have to be an increased scientific effort designed to institutionalize the IPCC work. Second, the rich industrialized countries would have to provide financial assistance and facilitate the transfer of technology to Third World countries. Third, countries would have to commit themselves to start taking measures for

---

17 See M. Paterson and M. Grubb, "The International Politics of Climate Change," *International Affairs*, April 1992.

reasons — such as general conservation activities — having nothing directly to do with global warming but that would still help reduce greenhouse gases.

In the crunch, the negotiations were naturally much more specific: How comprehensive should the convention be in terms of the greenhouse gases covered? What kinds of reduction targets should be set? What time frames should apply to such commitments? What funds would be needed for financial assistance? What concepts of equity should apply in burden sharing among countries?[18] As the discussions-*cum*-negotiations began in 1991, national divisions were apparent and complex, with most of the positions directly correlated with the political economy of each country's energy use.[19] But there were also divisions over the inherent economics of control options.[20]

The United States most opposed a climate convention, because of its profligate energy use, because of the 1991–92 recession, and because of the difficulty of mobilizing a domestic consensus in the light of the bruising environmental battle over amendments in 1990 to the *Clean Air Act*. Japan also appeared unwilling to move quickly, largely because it felt that it already had the world's most efficient energy use system and that others should achieve Japanese targets first. The positions of the EC countries varied, with the Nordic countries, The Netherlands, and West Germany, for example, advocating strong action, Spain, Greece, and Portugal seeking far less strict reductions, and Britain lodged somewhere in the middle. As mentioned earlier, these disputes were among the factors that led to the resignation of the EC Environment Commissioner just prior to

18 See M. Grubb and J.K. Sebenius, "Participation, Allocation and Adaptability in International Tradeable Emission Permit Systems for Greenhouse Gas Control" (Paper presented to an Organisation for Economic Co-operation and Development workshop, Paris, June 1991); and M. Grubb, D.G. Victor, and C. Hope, *Rethinking the Comprehensive Approach to Climate Change* (London: Royal Institute of International Affairs, November 1991).

19 See W.A. Nitze, *The Greenhouse Effect: Formulating a Convention* (London: Royal Institute of International Affairs, 1990), pp. 4–10.

20 See D. Pearce, "Economics and Global Environmental Protection," *Science and Public Affairs* 5 (1990): 67–73; and F. Cairncross, *Costing the Earth* (London: The Economist Books, 1991), ch. 7.

the Rio Earth Summit. Canada, Australia, and New Zealand all advocated strong action, but Canada's position was attacked by the Western Canadian oil and gas industry as well as by coal interests.

Canada's approach to the global warming issue began with some international position taking by Environment Minister Lucien Bouchard followed by an effort to coordinate its negotiating positions through a fairly elaborate consultative apparatus. The latter reflected the strong criticism that emerged from energy interests after the stand that Bouchard took on CO_2 at the Bergen meetings, which, in turn, came hard on the heels of the NOx Protocol misadventure.

DOE established a Climate Change Convention Negotiations Office in its Atmospheric Environmental Service. Advising the negotiators — a DOE-EAITC team headed by EAITC — were two advisory and consultative bodies, the Climate Change Convention Advisory Committee and the Provincial-Territorial Advisory Committee. The former was nominally intended to embrace both business and the ENGOs, but the ENGOs declined to be involved through this mechanism. In part their decision to opt out was due to their wish to concentrate on ensuring that domestic targets were met, but also because of their residual anger over the failure of the federal government to consult properly over the Green Plan. It was also a calculated decision that the ENGOs' best leverage lay in the combined circumstances of global warming and UNCED, in the massive use of public and media pressure, and in concert with other ENGOs around the world. One Quebec ENGO agreed to take part in the climate change advisory committee, but it was severely criticized by other ENGOs for breaking ranks. The ENGOs have formed, through the Canadian Environmental Network, a Climate Action Network Council to press hard for significant reductions rather than merely a stabilization of CO_2 emissions.

Accordingly, the advisory committee became mainly a consultative vehicle for business. Composed of about 20 knowledgeable persons drawn from the key sectors affected — namely, oil and gas, coal, utilities, mining, and pulp and paper — it met two weeks after each negotiating session and again one month prior to the next session. When requesting its negotiating authority from the Cabinet prior to each negotiating session, the negotiators agreed to submit the industry — as well as ENGO and provincial — positions as a part of their Cabinet submission. In addition, records of committee meetings were sent to ministers. An energy caucus within the committee also lobbied the energy minister hard, and he, too, was at the Cabinet table to influence negotiating positions.

The initial approach of the negotiating office within the Atmospheric Environmental Service was to give committee participants a series of papers on key issues. But these were often too general to be of interest to the business groups. Their interest was easily piqued, however, as soon as actual emissions and targets began to be discussed. Thus considerable business input occurred, which undoubtedly was an improvement over the NOx and Basle situations.

The Provincial-Territorial Advisory Committee was structured so that each province and territory would be represented by a dual delegation from its environment and energy departments. Again, the purpose of the committee was to keep the provinces abreast of the negotiations and to obtain provincial views about the negotiating position that Canada ought to be adopting. (Interestingly, the energy representatives took a greater interest in the process than did the environment people.) The provinces had all urged Canada to argue for a comprehensive approach that included all greenhouse gas rather than focusing only on CO_2, but they saw firsthand at the international meetings how Canada got only limited support for that position in the early negotiations. In general, the committee was not as active a group as its industrial counterpart because key energy provinces such as Alberta were exercising pressure through other ministers and departments, and because the impact of CO_2 emission reductions varies greatly among the provinces.

A further example of a more institutionalized approach to the Climate Change Convention process is that the Canadian scientific effort was channeled through a Canadian Climate Program Board aided by key scientific and technical input from the Canadian Climate Centre in DOE's Atmospheric Environmental Service.

A final, but vital, point can be made about the Climate Change Convention process. Unlike the cases of the Ozone Layer Convention and Montreal Protocol, where international bureaucratic entrepreneurs such as Mostafa Tolba took the initiative, the global warming issue had no equivalent leading player. This may be because the issue was much more complex in terms of the number and scale of interacting pollutants, the scale of uncertainty about the science and effects of greenhouse gases; the number of countries involved; the scale of potential conflict among countries and, equally, within countries; and its occurrence at a time of deep recession and the breakup of the Soviet bloc.

In the end, 154 states and the European Community signed the Climate Change Convention at the Rio Earth Summit. Under pressure from the United States, the convention was a framework agreement with no targets or schedules. A financial mechanism was put in place to satisfy the developing world, but the industrialized countries insisted it be viewed as an interim arrangement. The agreement accepts the notion of comprehensiveness in principle — in that all greenhouse gases eventually will be encompassed; in practice, the absence of targets and schedules makes this only a small victory for a position pushed hard by Canada and the Nordic countries. The convention does require immediate followup meetings and discussions and thus, like the Ozone Convention, it hopes to capitalize on the momentum that has built up. The major Canadian ENGOs stayed away from the consultative groups throughout and criticized the absence of targets and schedules, but they did not go out of their way on climate change issues to seek to embarrass their own government at Rio. For its part, industry — especially energy interests — heaved a sigh of relief that time had been bought before targets are set. They will, however, face a domestic commitment to stabilize emissions.

The New DOE-EAITC Pact

In Chapter 2, I set out the basis for the DOE-EAITC nexus in international environmental matters. I also noted the ups and downs of

EAITC's interest in environmental matters. This began with a heavy political involvement in the 1972 Stockholm Conference and its immediate aftermath, followed by a long period, extending well into the late 1980s, when environmental issues were simply not a high foreign or domestic policy priority of the Trudeau or Mulroney governments.[21]

All this changed in the wake of the difficulties experienced with the NOx Protocol and the Basle Convention. Environmental matters reached new political heights in the late 1980s with Prime Minister Mulroney attending a series of international meetings in which environmental issues were prominent on the agenda. By the early 1990s, EAITC was treating environmental issues on a par with development aid, disarmament issues, trade matters, and security concerns. Indeed, the foreign policy literature increasingly began to view environmental issues as part of the modern concept of international security.[22]

As EAITC sought to redefine its relationship with DOE in the new context of global environmental matters, it pointed out that while DOE had the scientific expertise, it could not compete with EAITC on security issues or with the Canadian International Development Agency on development assistance. Nor was DOE expert on patents and technology transfer issues that were the turf of other federal departments. Moreover, international environmental agreements such as the Montreal Protocol had begun to use trade policy as a compliance tool in ways that could contravene the rules of the General Agreement on Tariffs and Trade.[23] This was in EAITC's domain as well.

In the actual negotiation of agreements, EAITC claimed that its role as the repository of international legal expertise was more necessary than ever; there obviously is a legal dimension to such

---

21 See G.B. Doern and T. Conway, *The Greening of Canada: Twenty Years of Environmental Policy* (forthcoming, 1992), ch. 6.

22 See Mathews, "Redefining Security."

23 See K. Anderson and R. Blackhurst, eds., *The Greening of World Trade Issues* (London: Harvester Wheatsheaf, 1992), ch. 1.

agreements. Thus, EAITC's legal experts look for and seek to influence the structure of the agreement (preambles, definitions, operational articles), the clarity of the principles stated, the precision of entry-into-force provisions, and smoking guns or loophole clauses residing in annexes to the agreement. Arguments actually cut both ways on the role of legal expertise in the drafting of such treaties. For example, one of the arguments made by some players regarding the development of the Montreal Protocol was that the absence of lawyers early on was actually key to finding more flexible approaches to policy problems.

As noted earlier, EAITC had developed a new approach to environmental issues in the wake of the NOx and Basle difficulties. It included an abortive effort to construct a new consultative mechanism with business. This effort met with resistance from DOE and became linked to the larger turf wars in Ottawa during the time that the federal Green Plan was being forged in 1990. By late 1991, however, a new pact of sorts emerged that resulted in an improved process for handling environmental foreign policy. Interdepartmental rivalry, however, made it impossible to construct a formal Memorandum of Understanding between the two. Instead, a joint Memorandum to Cabinet helped to rationalize the core of the environmental foreign policy process. To facilitate the management of the process, Cabinet is now presented with an annual report on international environmental affairs. In addition, every international negotiating session must now be preceded by the receipt of a formal negotiating mandate from Cabinet. These steps were taken mainly to rationalize access to Green Plan funds, but also because, in some of the late 1980s' negotiating meetings, DOE refused to go to Cabinet to get negotiating mandates, nor was it necessarily required to.

Both DOE and EAITC are confident about the new approach. DOE officials see the new arrangements in the context of the department's own efforts to consolidate the internal decisionmaking process, including: a regular briefing of the Deputy Minister on all international issues; the decision to ensure that the Canadian Council of Ministers of the Environment is the means for informing the provinces about the international agenda and through which the provinces are to be consulted; and the work of the Friday Group to get an early warning system for business.

These arrangements do not capture all of the current or potential ways in which the DOE-EAITC nexus operates. The various regional and country desks of the two departments occasionally deal with environmental issues, for example, and they are an important part of the Canada-US relationship. A potential new source of tension undoubtedly will be the Cabinet requirement that all policies undergo prior environmental assessment. Nevertheless, a pact now exists between DOE and EAITC that is superior to the situation of the late 1980s. But the nexus between the two will never be entirely clear or stable since DOE is first and foremost an environmental department, whereas EAITC is unlikely to accord environmental issues a continuously high priority given its other roles and views of the world.

Conclusions

In the early 1990s, there was a quantum leap in the complexity of environmental foreign policy and in the difficulties involved in mobilizing domestic interests. The Bergen and Basle processes showed the continuing potential for environmental lightning bolts and the lack of full Canadian preparedness. The multisector approach adopted for the Bergen and UNCED meetings will become the norm, presenting tremendous challenges for Canada's business, ENGO, and government participants alike.

The decisionmaking process for the Climate Change Convention was innovative in that it involved the business community, but the ENGOs refused to join. Some learning was evident in the linkages between the Montreal Protocol approach and the approach used for global warming. Each hazard is different, however, and the lessons learned in dealing with one may not apply to another. Inevitably, a certain amount of consultative fatigue and frustration tends to set in when the same interests and players have to function in several arenas at once. The UNCED process, moreover, was so complex that it defies conventional generalizations, especially given its uniquely broad agenda and the remarkable media politics that accompanied the Rio Earth Summit.

There have also been important attempts to improve the core relationship between External Affairs and International Trade Canada and the Department of the Environment. A new *modus vivendi* is in evidence that is superior to the battles that occurred in the late 1980s. But environmental foreign policy will always be a struggle between a department (DOE) that ranks environmental values above all others and one (EAITC) that must accommodate related political, economic, and strategic issues.

Chapter 5

Green Diplomacy:
The Next Steps

In previous chapters, I examined the main issues and key players involved in international green decisionmaking. I also looked at the dynamics of the decisionmaking process regarding several important recent agreements, conventions, and protocols, with particular focus on the processes through which consensus among Canadian domestic interests was secured or conflict among them managed.

The notion of a "green" global decisionmaking process inherently involves the management of environmental and economic parameters to promote sustainable development. In the 1990s, this process is difficult because the sets of policy issues and imperatives involved are difficult to reconcile.

The ecological-economic policy issues center on how to manage situations where adverse environmental effects on third parties occur in part because of the absence of property rights and the improper pricing of environmental costs. These issues, in turn, are linked to problems of overpopulation in developing countries and profligate resource exploitation among rich Western countries.

The political-distributive dilemmas center around how to share equitably the burden of change among and within nations, between developing and developed countries, and intergenerationally. It also centers on how to establish politically legitimate institutions that are capable of negotiating complex agreements.

The managerial and organizational policy concerns center on how to design accountable international and related domestic institutions that have the requisite financial and scientific capacity to implement agreements effectively.

The decisionmaking process is also increasingly difficult because the players and institutions involved increase with the growing complexity and interdependence of hazards and pollutants. Moreover, the domestic and international players, both public and private, bring to the table varied sets of values and incentive systems. The process is not simply one of "government" or "interest groups" in some aggregate form. Rather, it involves numerous interests within the Canadian government, within and among provincial governments and international agencies, and within and among scientists, business, and environmental nongovernmental organizations (ENGOs). And these realities are replicated in every country that is involved in an international negotiation. Indeed, it is not at all clear that one can even properly speak of there being a single, recognizable international-domestic green decisionmaking process. The rudiments of a process seem to be evolving, but one of the striking features of the decisionmaking case studies is that various interests often simply do not agree on what process they are in, let alone on how well it may be working.

The dilemmas of forging domestic consensus and managing conflict within Canada are also a function of the five more particular issues posed at the outset of the study:

- the nature of international green agenda setting;
- the dynamics of, and difficulties involved in, determining the national interest in negotiations;
- the limits of domestic consensus formation, including the issue of "one stop" versus multi-arena lobbying by key business and ENGO stakeholders;
- the nature and extent of preparation in enabling effective provincial and interest group participation in national delegations; and
- the adequacy of the nexus between the Department of the Environment (DOE) and External Affairs and International Trade Canada (EAITC) in international environmental policy and decisionmaking for the rest of the 1990s.

In combination, these issues suggest final overall conclusions about whether each of the key players is doing all it can to enhance the coherence and ecological-economic balance of Canada's choices in international environmental decisionmaking.

International Green Agenda Setting

The nature of international green agenda setting has changed markedly in the past two decades. In the 1970s and early 1980s, it was a process in which a few fairly simple hazards arose at manageably spaced intervals. By the 1990s, it had evolved into one where many interactive and complex hazards and pollutants were on the agenda. Scientists are key players at the early stages of the agenda cycle and are increasingly institutionalized into the convention and protocol amendment process itself. Despite this vital technical presence, however, the subsequent movement of hazards up or down the international political priority list is certainly not determined by science alone. Much like the dynamics of earlier domestic environmental priority setting, the movement of issues toward an action-and-control stage is also intensely political and economic. In short, it is propelled by factors such as the balance of ENGO-business lobbying and pressure, the leadership or entrepreneurial policy role of key ministers or officials, and the mixture of both substantive and tactical scientific and technological controversy as to whether control technologies or substitute products are available or appropriate.

Canada has experienced the full gamut of these priority-setting dynamics and factors.[1] In the early cases involving sulfur dioxide (SO_2) and the Convention on Long-Range Transboundary Air Pollution, DOE's science was good — ahead of the game, in fact — and linked to appropriate control options. Being an international environmental leader also made sense because the main affected domestic interests were aware of what had to be done and could not argue

---

1 On overall environmental priority setting, see G.B. Doern and T. Conway, *The Greening of Canada: Twenty Years of Environmental Policy* (forthcoming, 1992), ch. 2.

that they were being taken by surprise. In the nitrogen oxide (NOx) case, the scientific and technical issues were less clear and DOE was too far ahead of the domestic interests most affected. The decision-making processes leading to the Rio Earth Summit and the Convention on Climate Change, building on the experience of the Basle Convention, were better than the early NOx process, but the scale of the issues at Rio was so great that it is difficult to judge the adequacy of these new complex processes. The fact is that the scale of the Rio exercise was unprecedented in terms of the number of interests involved and the complexity of the issues. The same applies to global warming, biodiversity, and forestry.

The case of the Vienna Convention for the Protection of the Ozone Layer and the subsequent Montreal Protocol warns that each hazard is very different. In this instance, the economic consequences to Canada, while not trivial, were relatively small compared to those of the SO_2 case, while the scale of global problems was serious indeed. Canada played a leadership and brokerage role in the international agenda, but this does not mean that Canada should lead only when the economic consequences are small or modest. It does suggest, however, that the priority-setting process and judgments of when to lead and when to follow are not easy.

The National Interest and Protocol Juggernauts

If the international green priority-setting process is, at best, semirational and if different hazards evoke vastly different arrays of interests, then Canada has a serious problem in determining its national interest. Should it lead, slow down, or broker protocol "juggernauts" — international environmental initiatives that develop a global momentum Canada's decisionmakers cannot ignore — when they emerge on the world green agenda? The suddenness or speed of these initiatives means that every country can get caught up in the media game of pointing fingers at environmental laggards.

Clearly, no country has a monopoly on green sin or green virtue, and there are no iron-clad norms or tactical rules to rely on for each case.

The notion of what the national interest is in such circumstances is also conceptually imposing. Does the national interest reside in being a good citizen of the planet? Is it to allow a country's worst polluters the time to change their ways while ensuring their future competitiveness? Is it to ensure that a neighboring country acts first, because no matter what Canada can do domestically the problem cannot be solved without major action abroad?

Some environmentalists argue that, on these increasingly global environmental issues, there is no such thing as the national interest, that we are all custodians of the global commons. In some respects, this is undoubtedly true. This position cannot be sustained in practice for long, however, because international solutions necessarily consist of an aggregated mix of national resource and allocative decisions. Thus, ways must be found to determine that Canada's environment-economy decisionmakers are, in fact, making decisions that reflect a flexible approach to changing cases, pollutants, and hazards.

At first glance, the only way to be confident that one has a handle on an agreed notion of the national interest may be to have the right processes in place. According to this view, the national interest is really just the result of a bargain struck by the various domestic players who, in turn, are being buffeted by a series of international pressures. In short, the whole process seems to be a pluralist balance-of-power outcome.

While such process-based criteria are undoubtedly a large part of what the national interest is at any given moment, they are certainly not all there is to it. There is also a vital substantive aspect to the national (and international) public interest in reaching international agreements on the environment. Inevitably and unavoidably, these substantive aspects take decisionmakers back to the main policy issues and the questions or criteria they imply: Will the contemplated actions in fact reduce or eliminate the environmental hazard? Is Canada's share of that solution a reasonable one given the physical attributes of that hazard within Canada and in the world? Will the mechanisms of control and product substitution allow the Canadian economy to carry them out effectively and efficiently so as to ease economic adjustment and ensure that Canadian industries can compete? Will the instruments be employed so as to have as many resources as possible left over for other social and economic issues, including further progress on upcoming green hazards?

These substantive policy criteria are always hazard specific. They require good science and good analysis as well as stakeholder processes that are open not just democratically but also in the sense that they are capable of making the detailed examination of technical and economic analysis easier.

The Limits of Domestic Consensus Formation

However much international-domestic green decisionmaking processes have improved in recent years, the case studies show that there are very real limitations on how far domestic consensus formation can go.

The first limitation arises out of the simple fact that there are substantive conflicts among the interests involved. The leading government agency, other government agencies, particular provinces, industries, and ENGOs all have different interests and priorities. Sometimes, they simply cannot agree because they are defending different material interests.

The second limitation to consensus formation is that interests often do not agree on what the appropriate decision process ought to be, or whether there ought to be only one process. These limits, in turn, are linked to the different procedural or tactical approaches adopted by the main players, as well as the inherent difference between an elected government and unelected interest groups. The latter usually want to preserve their right to lobby in the decision-making arenas and pressure points of their own choosing. Interest group stakeholders, especially business and ENGOs, may want

Canada's negotiating positions to be synonymous with their own, but it is, of course, a democratic fact of some importance that interest groups are not elected to govern. Only the government of the day is, and, in this case, the federal government's positions are most frequently represented by DOE and EAITC as the main makers of environmental foreign policy. In the final analysis, it is the government, through its ministers and negotiators, that must interpret the national interest and act on it.

For their part, key interest groups such as business and ENGOs, often practice a tactical double standard when commenting on the adequacy of the international environmental decisionmaking process. If the government's substantive position does not reflect theirs, they may simply regard the consultation process as flawed, rather than recognizing that there may be honest differences of opinion. At the same time, interest groups will almost always want to reserve the right to lobby in whatever arena of power they choose *in addition* to the formal channel of consensus formation that may have been devised for a particular hazard or occasion. ENGOs, for example, tend to criticize and embarrass the government in the media even when they are accorded considerable participation in the formal international process. Similarly, business will seek out other economic ministers and bureaucracies to do their bidding for them.

These realities account for much of the dissatisfaction with the domestic consultative and decisionmaking process, but not for all of it. Other substantive grievances about the nature of the international green decisionmaking process have had a considerable basis in fact. Hence, greater confidence needs to be fostered in the way national delegations are prepared for international negotiations.

Fostering Greater Confidence in the Delegation-Preparation Process

The NOx and Basle cases showed that there was some merit in business and provincial criticism of the failure to have even the minimum mechanisms in place for notifying special interest groups of events and decisions that would affect them. There were also problems in the early decisionmaking process on the Climate Change Convention, when its advisory committee was hit with a flurry of bureaucratic papers. The ENGOs in the Bergen preparation process were frustrated by the focus on paperflow contact rather than face-to-face meetings with potential delegates.

Recent reforms have addressed some of the early notification issues and position taking by ministers without consultation with affected interests. The actual extent of personal contact among delegates in the preparation process is, however, still quite small. But to appreciate the options here, one must deal again with the nature of international negotiations. Three of their key features warrant a final mention.

First, if there is to be an improved consensus, the affected domestic interests must be able to trust the DOE-EAITC negotiators and what they are likely to say in the negotiating room. This, in turn, means that they have reasonable confidence in the negotiating mandate given by the Cabinet prior to the meetings and that the mandate has been based to some significant extent on the Cabinet's awareness of their position. It means that the letters of instruction to the delegates similarly evoke their concerns.

Second, the fostering of this kind of enhanced consensus is inevitably connected to the realities of complex international negotiations. As the case studies have shown, negotiations are joint decisionmaking processes in which at least some key players can exercise an actual or partial veto by walking away. They are, in effect, exercises in political power.[2] The process centers on efforts to influence the location of a settlement point in a potential zone of agreement. But none of the parties can identify that point precisely in advance because each has very imperfect information about the preferences of other players. Because of this inner dynamic, one has to experience the process to know and understand what happened. But because a deal may result that one can later compare with

---

2 See H. Raiffa, *The Art and Science of Negotiation* (Cambridge, Mass.: Harvard University Press, 1982).

hypothetical alternatives, there are always plenty of armchair quarterbacks on the morning after the game. Indeed, in environmental politics, the quarterbacks work the whole week and refuse to see themselves as mere spectators!

Third, international green negotiations are increasingly like those surrounding the General Agreement on Tariffs and Trade (GATT) or other complex talks. They do not take place in one cozy room; numerous country delegations meet in plenary sessions; many working groups are struck along subject matter lines; coalitions are struck along regional or ideological lines. Eventually, however, negotiations do come down to a smaller set of players who usually consist of the host country or sponsoring green agency, key world powers, and regional representatives, with the odd other honest-broker country thrown in. Canada may or may not be in this inner circle. The access of any Canadian delegation of federal, provincial, business, and ENGO representatives may first be to the head of delegation (from EAITC or DOE), but the latter may or may not be in the inner room.

Thus, a compelling overall feature of such complex negotiations is the personal network of trust that has to be fostered within any Canadian delegation and among other delegations as well. It is a people-intensive process. Yet the evidence to date suggests that Canada's international teams have little time to forge such personal links; the prior preparation is almost entirely a paperflow approach.

There is, then, much more room for personal trust-building dialogue, but the practical problems are considerable. Delegates are busy people and scheduling face-to-face meetings is difficult. Cost is another considerable barrier. Governmental participants are also reluctant to trust interest-group delegates who may use the media to criticize their own country. In this regard, international green negotiations are somewhat different from the GATT or other complex negotiations in that ENGOs, aided by intense media coverage, represent a kind of surrogate expression of world public opinion. In the final analysis, however, the government is the actual negotiator and will catch the political flak if things go wrong.

The DOE-EAITC Duo and the Economy-Environment Connection

It is clear that, in all policy fields, international imperatives are becoming important.[3] Thus, Canada must get its act together to do deals with the rest of the world. The DOE-EAITC nexus within the government of Canada is crucial in the making of environmental foreign policy and in forging a domestic consensus. The two departments have begun to learn from earlier green negotiations and have improved and institutionalized the decisionmaking process in a number of ways. These include the requirement that the departments obtain negotiating mandates from Cabinet and that they submit annual reports on such negotiations and agreements; the identification of the Canadian Council of Ministers of the Environment as the main federal-provincial forum for international environmental matters; the formation of the business Friday Group; and the overall effort to involve stakeholders in the complex Rio Earth Summit and Climate Change Convention decisionmaking processes.

The two lead players have not, however, entirely broken away from their past foreign policymaking habits. For DOE, a key part of its 20-year history has been the desire to do good in the international environmental world by showing environmental leadership. For EAITC, the functional equivalent has been the equally proud Pearsonian traditions of peacekeeper and middle-power broker and fixer.

Both departments have had economic roles thrust upon them only in the relatively recent past. For EAITC, a key change came in the early 1980s, when it took on new trade policy responsibilities. For DOE, the change began in the latter part of the 1980s, when it became involved with environment-economy policy exercises such as the Brundtland process and the Green Plan. Both departments wear these new economic mantles uncomfortably, their past traditions more often than not overruling their new obligations.

---

3 See G.B. Doern and R.W. Phidd, *Canadian Public Policy: Ideas, Structure, Process*, 2nd ed. (Toronto: Nelson, 1992), ch. 14 and 17.

The departments increasingly understand their new roles, but not to the extent that they have been able to develop a medium or long-term strategy to deal with international environmental relations as a dual ecological and economic set of choices. If Canada hopes to promote a greener world while defending its national interest in a complex international environmental and economic agenda, then its capacity to bring the majority of domestic interests on side in international negotiations still has a long way to go.

The Players' Obligations and Future Environmental Diplomacy

A major struggle is under way among the players in the game of green diplomacy to cope with new realities. They make progress with each new challenge they face and with each new approach they try, but there is still much they can do to improve Canada's diplomatic efforts on the environmental front.

For the federal government, it is likely that environmental diplomacy will have to move beyond DOE and EAITC in at least two senses. First, the Canadian International Development Agency — which is a part of EAITC — and its development assistance funding will increasingly be a part of the political and economic equation. Second, the Department of Finance will have to become a more active player. In both cases, the compelling reason is that the government is likely to face potentially large financial obligations: special incremental development funding and technology transfer funding are increasingly a part of international environmental diplomacy. But so far there is little sense that the government knows what these costs will be or where the money will come from. While clearly aware of these problems, neither EAITC or DOE is sufficiently economically oriented to be a credible defender of the economics and financing of these potentially open-ended obligations.

For Canadian business, the challenge in future negotiations is to move beyond generalized complaints about the real and alleged failures of consultation to a more realistic appreciation of the complexity both of the processes involved and of the positions of its component parts. If current processes are inadequate, business will have to suggest constructive alternatives. It will also have to seek more institutionalized links — undoubtedly in concert with international business organizations — with international environmental agencies, as have ENGOs. Business positions, while quite properly focusing on economic concerns and the real costs to the Canadian economy, will also have to recognize the economic opportunities that arise from using the best international environmental practices. Business coalitions are no longer monolithic sources of resistance to environmental change because key firms within any given sector may see strategic economic advantage for themselves in supporting tougher international standards.

For ENGOs, the challenge of environmental diplomacy is as sobering as it is for business. Increasingly, they need to stretch their resources into many arenas of negotiation. However rhetorically satisfying it may be in the short run to bash one's own government in these complex negotiations, it is highly unlikely to be the best strategy in the long run. ENGOs will have to work closely with business and government if Canada's sustainable development needs are to be properly addressed in a world process where this country is just one of many players. Some ENGOs realize this; those that do not will find themselves on the outside looking in.

Provincial governments face realities that are a miniature replica of those confronting Ottawa. They have their own divisions between environment and economic departments, and special concerns when dominant regional industries are perceived to be at risk. But they also have their share of environmental industries and ENGOs pressing for change. The multilateral federal-provincial machinery for international environmental negotiations has improved somewhat in recent years. It still requires far more bilateral subtlety, however, since no two provinces face the same set of environmental-economic consequences from the complex issues that are on the international green agenda.

Last, but hardly least, there is the issue of how the scientific and technical community can improve its role. Although subject to political pressures and periodic "hired-gun" science, the scientific and technical role is the best buffer against an overly politicized decision-making process. Steps need to be taken to institutionalize the independence and openness of the scientific work that underpins international protocols and agreements. This is needed both within the federal and provincial governments but also through greater support for international technical bodies and for independent, university-based centers in Canada.

More generally, increased face-to-face contacts can improve the delegate preparation process. This would foster greater confidence and generate a better understanding of the constraints that negotiators face at the table. The process centers on mutual trust, however, and so it is incumbent on the government to consult, carefully and openly, key interests and to take their views seriously into account. Equally, private interests, in all fairness, have to resist the urge to take shots at their own government if they have been given an opportunity to participate in the negotiation preparation process. Solidarity among the delegates would strengthen Canada's negotiating position.

The post–Rio Earth Summit period will require a continuing effort to find ways to maximize trust and a sense of partnership with key domestic interests. Future work on global warming, biodiversity, and forestry, among many other environmental items, will generate considerable political and economic conflict within Canada. The players have no time to waste in learning what the new green game is all about.

Appendix 1

Chronology of Key International Environmental Events and Agreements

1972   Club of Rome publishes *The Limits to Growth*.

United Nations sponsors the Stockholm Conference on the Human Environment.

United Nations Environmental Programme (UNEP) established.

Convention on the Prevention of Marine Pollution by Dumping of Wastes and Other Matter (London Dumping Convention) signed.

Convention for the Protection of the World's Cultural and Natural Heritage signed in Paris.

Convention on the Conservation of Antarctic Seals signed.

1973   International Convention for the Prevention of Pollution from Ships signed.

Convention on International Trade in Endangered Species of Wild Fauna and Flora signed.

1977   UNEP's Ad Hoc Conference of Experts endorses World Plan of Action on the Ozone Layer.

1979	Convention on Long-Range Transboundary Air Pollution (LRTAP) signed.
1980	World Conservation Strategy initiated jointly by UNEP and the International Union for the Conservation of Nature and Natural Resources.
1982	United Nations Convention on the Law of the Sea signed.
1985	Helsinki Protocol (to the LRTAP) on Sulfur Dioxide signed.
	Vienna Convention for the Protection of the Ozone Layer signed.
	Villach Conference of climate experts produces consensus on serious possibility of global warming.
1986	Major nuclear accident occurs at Chernobyl, Ukraine.
1987	Montreal Protocol on Substances that Deplete the Ozone Layer signed.
	World Commission on Environment and Development (the Brundtland Commission) publishes *Our Common Future*.
1988	Sofia Protocol (to the LRTAP) on Nitrogen Oxides (NOx) signed.
	Intergovernmental Panel on Climate Change established by the World Meteorological Organization and UNEP.

Leaders of the Group of Seven (G-7) major industrialized countries endorse the concept of sustainable development at the Toronto Summit.

1989   Basle Convention on the Control of Transboundary
            Movements of Hazardous Wastes and Their Dis-
            posal signed.

            Noordwijk Declaration by Ministerial Conference
            on Atmospheric Pollution and Climate Change sets
            out commitment to stabilize carbon dioxide emis-
            sions by 2000.

            United Nations commits to holding a Conference
            on Environment and Development (UNCED) in
            1992 in Rio de Janiero, Brazil.

1990   Parties to the Montreal Protocol meet in London to
            strengthen the Protocol.

            G-7 leaders at the Houston Summit call for negoti-
            ations to begin to develop an agreement on the
            world's forests.

            United Nations Economic Commission for Europe
            sponsors Bergen Conference to follow up the agenda
            of the Brundtland Commission's report on sustain-
            able development; Ministerial Declaration calls for
            stabilization of carbon dioxide emissions.

1991   Negotiations on an international climate change
            convention begin.

            Negotiations on a biodiversity convention begin.

1992   UNCED is held in Rio with massive world media
            coverage.

United Nations Framework Convention on Climate Change is signed at Rio.

United Nations Biodiversity Convention is signed at Rio.

Declaration of Principles on Forests is signed at Rio.

World political leaders sign Rio Declaration, setting out major principles of sustainable development.

Rio meeting endorses Agenda 21, setting out a massive array of economic and environmental actions for the twenty-first century.

Appendix 2

Key Events in the Decisionmaking Process on Long-Range Transboundary Air Pollution (LRTAP), Sulfur Dioxide (SO₂), and Nitrogen Oxides (NOx)

Early 1970s	LRTAP Committee of the Organisation for Economic Co-operation and Development formed.
	Research in Nordic countries identifies SO_2 and acid rain problems and hazards, while Canada's Great Lakes atmospheric research shows hazards for this country.
May 1975	US symposium shows seriousness of acid rain problem in North America.
1976	Canada's Department of the Environment (DOE) establishes LRTAP program.
	Science Council of Canada releases *Policies and Poisons* study, which includes an examination of the acid rain problem.
1978	US congressional resolution concerning acid rain pollution from Canada leads the two countries to form a Bilateral Research Consultation Group.

1979	Geneva Convention on LRTAP negotiated, but lacks a commitment to reduce emissions.
1980	Canada and Carter Administration in the United States sign Memorandum of Intent to take concrete steps on acid rain.
	Coalition Against Acid Rain formed as Canadian environmental nongovernmental organization to lobby in Washington and domestically.
June 1982	Canada-US talks on acid rain break down due to opposition from Reagan Administration.
1983–84	Canada forges the "30 Percent Club," an international coalition committed to reducing SO_2 emissions by at least 30 percent by 1993 (Ottawa had already agreed to a domestic reduction of 50 percent by 1994).
	Joint business-government study of Canadian mining and smelting industry carried out linking new technologies, the post-recession competitive situation, and environmental issues.
February 1985	Ottawa and six provinces announce SO_2 control program; package of financial incentives made available because of importance of upcoming "Shamrock Summit" between Prime Minister Mulroney and President Reagan.
July 1985	Helsinki Protocol on SO_2 negotiated; Britain and the United States refuse to sign.

Fall 1986   Several European countries take steps to develop stricter standards for NOx emissions after research shows damage to forests and after pressure and electoral success by Green parties.

Nordic countries press Canada to join new "30 Percent Club".

Canadian science on forest effects inconclusive in part because of Canada's greater interest in NOx, which combines with volatile organic compounds (VOCs) to produce ground-level ozone.

1987–88   Canada, led by DOE, presses for NOx Protocol, in part to keep up pressure on the United States on the larger bilateral LRTAP agenda; DOE presses for critical-loads concept for protocol regime rather than across-the-board cuts.

Environmentalists use media pressure to prompt Ontario publicly to urge Ottawa to join the 30 Percent Club.

October 1988   Canada and 24 other countries sign the Sofia Protocol to freeze NOx emissions at 1987 levels, to apply to new sources the best available technology that is economically feasible, and to establish further measures to solve NOx-related environmental problems by 1996.

Canadian Council of Ministers of the Environment (CCME) launches stakeholder process to develop national management plan to control NOx-VOCs emissions.

1988–89   Some provinces and businesses, especially in the energy sector, express severe criticism of NOx Protocol process; criticism eventually linked to entire process and substance of the federal Green Plan and related problems with the Basle Convention on Hazardous Wastes.

1990   United States, under the Bush Administration, finally takes action on the SO_2 issue with the passage of the *Clean Air Act*.

1991   VOCs Protocol signed, with Canada's position worked out within context of CCME NOx-VOCs Management Plan.

Appendix 3

Key Events in the Ozone Convention and Montreal Protocol Decisionmaking Process

1974
Research shows implications of ozone layer depletion by manmade chemicals such as chlorofluorocarbons (CFCs).

1976–78
Canada, the United States, and Sweden ban the use of CFCs in aerosols. Canadian regulations take effect in 1980.

1977
United Nations Environmental Programme (UNEP) establishes Coordinating Committee on the Ozone Layer.

1982
UNEP establishes working group to develop draft framework for a convention. Stalemate develops between the United States and European Community (EC) countries over control action, with the EC countries and chemical companies fearful that US firms would capture their market share during the transition from CFCs to substitute products.

1984
Lawsuit brought in the United States by Natural Resources Defense Council leads to court order requiring US Environmental Protection Agency to

develop regulations on CFCs by 1987 or to explain why it had not done so.

1985   Vienna Convention on the Ozone Layer negotiated, with Canada playing lead broker role. Contains commitment to develop control program by 1987.

1985–87   UNEP establishes two working groups, one on scientific issues and one on control options. Canada plays key role on second committee in particular. The United States is key player on science coordinated through National Aeronautics and Space Administration (NASA).

September 1986 Meeting in Leesburg, Virginia, of UNEP's second working group involves multisector participation by environmental nongovernmental organizations (ENGOs), business, and scientists; probably the first time US ENGOs are directly involved in an international meeting; flexible control options are discussed based on initial Canadian proposals by DOE.

September 1987 Montreal Protocol signed; signatories commit to freeze use and production of CFCs at 1986 levels and to make cuts of a further 50 percent by 2000.

1987–88   NASA releases new data showing a stunning increase in the size of a hole in the ozone layer above Antarctica.

              A US firm, E.I. du Pont de Nemours & Co., the world's largest producer of CFCs, announces plans to phase out all production of CFCs and halons by 2000 and to invest heavily in product substitutes; Canada's two biggest producers, Du Pont of Canada and Allied Chemical, have little choice but to stop their opposition to Canada's control program. Du Pont Canada is better prepared with product substitutes due to its superior research and development, but the actions of the two firms anger competitors and split the industry lobby.

June 1988   Under the auspices of the Montreal Protocol, UNEP creates panels on Ecological and Human Adverse Effects of Ozone Layer Depletion; the Technical Feasibility of Increasing the Stringency and Scope of the Treaty; and Economic Impacts.

June 1989   A report by UNEP's Technical Panel discusses the technical and economic feasibility of increasing the scope and stringency of the Montreal Protocol.

1989   A broad coalition of over 90 ENGOs from 27 countries convenes in London to press for further reductions in emissions of CFCs and halons.

1990   62 signatories of the Montreal Protocol agree to amend the Protocol to provide for stricter controls and to establish a multilateral fund to assist Third World countries with financing and technology transfer.

Selected Bibliography

Anderson, K., and R. Blackhurst, eds. *The Greening of World Trade Issues.* London: Harvester Wheatsheaf, 1992.

Barratt-Brown, E.P. "Building a Monitoring and Compliance Regime under the Montreal Protocol," *Yale Journal of International Law* 16 (1990).

Barrett, S. "The Problem of Global Environmental Protection," *Oxford Review of Economic Policy* 6 (1990).

Benedick, R.E. "Lessons from the Ozone Hole," *EPA Journal* 16 (March-April 1990).

———. *Ozone Diplomacy: New Directions in Safeguarding the Planet.* Cambridge, Mass.: Harvard University Press, 1991.

Boehmer-Christiansen, S. *Acid Politics.* London: Oxford University Press, 1990.

Buxton, G.V. "UNCED and Lessons from the Montreal Protocol," *Law and Contemporary Problems* (forthcoming, 1992).

———; A. Chisolm; and J. Carbonneau. "A Canadian Contribution to the Consideration of Strategies for Protecting the Ozone Layer." Paper presented at the UNEP Workshop on Economic Issues Related to Control of CFCs, Leesburg, Virginia, September 8–12, 1986.

Cairncross, F. *Costing the Earth.* London: The Economist Books, 1991.

Caldwell, L.K. *International Environmental Policy.* 2nd ed. Durham, N.C.: Duke University Press, 1990.

Canada. *Canada's Green Plan.* Ottawa: Supply and Services Canada, 1990.

———. *Canada's Non-Ferrous Metals Industry: Nickel and Copper.* Ottawa: Supply and Services Canada, 1984.

———. Department of the Environment. International Affairs Branch. *International Environmental Issues: A Status Report.* Ottawa, 1990.

———. Parliament. House of Commons. Standing Committee on Fisheries and Forestry. Sub-Committee on Acid Rain. *Still Waters.* Ottawa: Supply and Services Canada, 1981.

———. Parliament. House of Commons. Standing Committee on Fisheries and Forestry. Sub-Committee on Acid Rain. *Time Lost: Demand for Action on Acid Rain.* Ottawa: Supply and Services Canada, 1984.

Dewees, D. "The Regulation of Sulphur Dioxide in Ontario." In G.B. Doern, ed. *Getting It Green: Case Studies in Canadian Environmental Regulation.* Toronto: C.D. Howe Institute, 1990.

Doern, G.B. *The Peripheral Nature of Scientific Controversy in Federal Policy Formation.* Ottawa: Science Council of Canada, 1981.

———. "Regulations and Incentives: The NOx-VOCs Case." In G.B. Doern, ed. *Getting It Green: Case Studies in Canadian Environmental Regulation.* Toronto: C.D. Howe Institute, 1990.

———. *Regulatory and Jurisdictional Issues in the Regulation of Hazardous Substances in Canada.* Ottawa: Science Council of Canada, 1977.

———. *Shades of Green: Gauging Canada's Green Plan,* C.D. Howe Institute Commentary 29. Toronto: C.D. Howe Institute, 1991.

———, and T. Conway. *The Greening of Canada: Twenty Years of Environmental Policy.* Forthcoming, 1992.

———, and R.W. Phidd. *Canadian Public Policy: Ideas, Structure, Process.* 2nd ed. Toronto: Nelson, 1992.

Ecological Impact of Acid Precipitation. Proceedings of a conference held at Sandefjord, Norway, March 11, 1980.

Enders, A., and A. Porges. "Successful Conventions and Conventional Success: Saving the Ozone Layer." In K. Anderson and R. Blackhurst, eds. *The Greening of World Trade Issues.* London: Harvester Wheatsheaf, 1992.

Gibson, R.B. "Out of Control and Beyond Understanding: Acid Rain as a Political Dilemma." In R. Paehlke and D. Torgerson, eds. *Managing Leviathan.* Peterborough: Broadview Press, 1990.

Grubb, M. *The Greenhouse Effect: Negotiating Targets.* London: Royal Institute of International Affairs, 1989.

———, and J.K. Sebenius. "Participation, Allocation and Adaptability in International Tradeable Emission Permit Systems for Greenhouse Gas Control." Paper presented to an Organisation for Economic Co-operation and Development workshop, Paris, June, 1991.

———; D.G. Victor; and C. Hope. *Rethinking the Comprehensive Approach to Climate Change.* London: Royal Institute of International Affairs, November 1991.

Hampson, F.O. "Climate Change and Global Warming: The Elusive Search for an International Convention." Maxwell School of Public Affairs Occasional Paper. Syracuse, N.Y.: Syracuse University, December 1990.

————. "New Wine in Old Bottles: The International Politics of the Environment." Paper presented to the Conference on the New World Situation and the Future of Peace, Hobart and William Smith Colleges, Geneva, New York, April 27, 1991.

Hare, K. "Environmental Uncertainty: Science and the Greenhouse Effect." In G.B. Doern, ed. *The Environmental Imperative: Market Approaches to the Greening of Canada.* Toronto: C.D. Howe Institute, 1990.

Hoberg, G. "Sleeping with an Elephant: The American Influence on Canadian Environmental Regulation." Paper prepared for the American Political Science Association Meetings, August 30, 1990, Mimeographed.

Howlett, M. "The Roundtable Experience: Representation and Legitimacy in Canadian Environmental Policymaking," *Queen's Quarterly* 97 (Winter 1990).

Jaeger, J., et al. *Developing Policies for Responding to Climate Change.* Stockholm: Beijer Institute and World Meteorological Organization, April 1988.

Kyba, P. "International Environmental Relations: Twenty Years of Canadian Involvement." Guelph, Ont., University of Guelph, 1990, Mimeographed.

Lang, W. "From Vienna to Montreal and Beyond: The Politics of Ozone Layer Protection." Vienna, 1989, Mimeographed.

————. "Negotiations on the Environment." Vienna, 1989, Mimeographed.

Lewis, D., and W. Davis. *Joint Report of the Special Envoys on Acid Rain.* Ottawa: Supply and Services Canada, January 1986.

Long Range Transport of Air Pollutants Steering Committee. *Management Plan for Nitrogen Oxides and Volatile Organic Compounds.* Ottawa, March 1990.

MacNeill, J., and R. Munro. "Environment 1972–1992: From the Margin to the Mainstream," *Ecodecision* 1 (Spring 1991).

Mathews, J.T., ed. *Preserving the Global Environment.* London: W.W. Norton, 1991.

————. "Redefining Security," *Foreign Affairs* 68 (Spring 1989).

Munton, D. "Dependence and Interdependence in Transboundary Environmental Relations," *International Journal* 36 (1980–81).

Newbery, D.M. "Acid Rain," *Economic Policy* 5 (October 1990).

Nitze, W.A. *The Greenhouse Effect: Formulating a Convention.* London: Royal Institute of International Affairs, 1990.

Nossal, K. *The Politics of Canadian Foreign Policy.* 2nd ed. Scarborough, Ont.: Prentice-Hall of Canada, 1989.

Organisation for Economic Co-operation and Development. *The OECD Programme on Long Range Transport of Air Pollutants.* Paris, 1977.

Park, C. *Acid Rain: Rhetoric and Reality.* New York: Methuen/Routledge, 1989.

Paterson, M., and M. Grubb. "The International Politics of Climate Change," *International Affairs,* April 1992.

Pearce, D. "Economics and Global Environmental Protection," *Science and Public Affairs* 5 (1990).

———. "Economics and the Global Environmental Challenge," *Millennium,* December 1990.

Pinder, J. *European Community.* Oxford: Oxford University Press, 1991.

Porter, G., and J.W. Brown. *Global Environmental Politics.* Boulder, Col.: Westview Press, 1991.

Raiffa, H. *The Art and Science of Negotiation.* Cambridge, Mass.: Harvard University Press, 1982.

Regens, J.L., and R.W. Rycroft. *The Acid Rain Controversy.* Pittsburgh: University of Pittsburgh Press, 1988.

Regional Conference on the Follow-up to the World Commission on Environment and Development in the ECE Region. *Action for a Common Future.* Bergen, Norway, May 8–16, 1990.

Sands, P., and J. Cameron. *International Law of Atmospheric Protection: A Critique of the Existing Rules.* London: Centre for International Environmental Law, 1990.

Schmidheiny, S., with the Business Council for Sustainable Development. *Changing Course.* Cambridge, Mass.: MIT Press, 1992.

Schneider, Stephen H. *Global Warming.* New York: Vintage Books, 1990.

Science Council of Canada. *Policies and Poisons.* Ottawa, 1977.

Sebenius, S.H. "Negotiating a Regime to Control Global Warming." Cambridge, Mass.: Harvard University, Kennedy School of Government, 1990.

Skogstad, G. "Environmental Policy in a Federal System: Ottawa and the Provinces." Paper prepared for the University of Toronto, Toronto, 1991.

Skolnikoff, E.B. "The Policy Gridlock on Global Warming," *Foreign Policy* 79 (Summer 1990).

Smith, D.A. "The Implementation of Policies to Protect the Ozone Layer." In G.B. Doern, ed. *Getting It Green: Case Studies in Canadian Environmental Regulation.* Toronto: C.D. Howe Institute, 1990.

Toner, G. "The Canadian Environmental Movement: A Conceptual Map." Paper prepared for Carleton University, Ottawa, 1991.

————. "Passionate Politics: Canada's Green Plan for Social Change," *Ecodecision* 1 (Spring 1991).

Vogel, D. *National Styles of Regulation: Environmental Policy in Great Britain and the United States.* Ithaca, N.Y.: Cornell University Press, 1986.

World Commission on Environment and Development. *Our Common Future,* chaired by Norwegian Prime Minister Gro Harlem Brundtland. Oxford: Oxford University Press, 1987.

Young, O.Y. *International Cooperation: Building Regimes for Natural Resources and the Environment.* Ithaca, N.Y.: Cornell University Press, 1989.

Members of the
C.D. Howe Institute[*]

[*] The views expressed in this publication are those of the author and do not necessarily reflect
    the opinions of the Institute's members.

The Toronto Stock Exchange
TransAlta Utilities Corporation
TransCanada PipeLines Limited
Trimac
Trizec Corporation Ltd.
Robert J. Turner
Unilever Canada Inc.
Univa Inc.
Urgel Bourgie Limitée
Manon Vennat
VIA Rail Canada Inc.

J.H. Warren
West Fraser Timber Co. Ltd.
Westcoast Energy Inc.
George Weston Limited
Alfred G. Wirth
M.K. Wong & Associates Ltd.
Wood Gundy Limited
Fred R. Wright
Xerox Canada Inc.
Zurich Life Insurance of Canada

Honorary Members

G. Arnold Hart
David Kirk
Paul H. Leman

A.M. Runciman
J. Ross Tolmie, Q.C.